Frank and Catherine have been friends of mine for years. They are uniquely gifted to present the healing power of God's Word in the context of real-life issues. They love people, and they're passionate for others to discover extraordinary personal freedom from their past. Their ministry has literally transformed countless lives all over the world. This book will transform you!

DR. GARY D. KINNAMAN
Author and Pastor to Pastors

Catherine and Frank Fabiano have written a very useful book and a worthy addition to the growing literature dealing with inner healing. They have taken the expertise provided by their professional training in developmental psychology and integrated it with the insights and effectiveness of inner healing. They demonstrate and teach how to bring emotional and spiritual healing to those struggling with issues arising from conception through adulthood. Though there are now several good inner-healing books in print, this is one of the best. I highly recommend it for practitioners and for those struggling with emotional and spiritual problems.

DR. CHARLES H. KRAFT
Author of *Deep Wounds, Deep Healing* and *Defeating Dark Angels*

The journey to uncovering buried pain can seem like an uninvited interruption, but it is completely necessary if one is to laugh easily and love life. In *Healing Your Past, Releasing Your Future*, the Fabianos use real-life stories and vast knowledge to help us learn to embrace God's complete healing for our past wounds and disarm the lodged memories that hold us captive. This book is an excellent and engaging resource for individuals, parents and ministers who truly desire to live out their true limitless heritage as children of God.

BOB AND AUDREY MEISNER
Bestselling Authors of *Marriage Under Cover*
TV Hosts of *My New Day*

This book is an absolute *must read*. This is our most-loved book apart from the Bible. Frank and Catherine's teaching, insight and practices have brought profound, deep healing. In just a few years we have seen more breakthroughs than in all the other years combined. Hundreds of our people have met Jesus and been set free to enjoy the future through this material with the power of the Holy Spirit.

JACKIE PULLINGER
Founder of St. Stephen's Society, Hong Kong

Healing
YOUR PAST
Releasing
YOUR
FUTURE

CATHERINE CAHILL FABIANO, M.S.
& FRANK P. FABIANO, M.S.

Chosen

a division of Baker Publishing Group
Minneapolis, Minnesota

© 2012 Frank P. Fabiano and Catherine Cahill Fabiano.

Published by Chosen Books
11400 Hampshire Avenue South
Bloomington, Minnesota 55438
www.chosenbooks.com

Chosen Books is a division of
Baker Publishing Group, Grand Rapids, Michigan

Chosen Books edition published 2014
ISBN 978-0-8007-9647-1

Previously published by Regal Books

Printed in the United States of America

The Library of Congress has cataloged the original edition as follows:
Fabiano, Catherine Cahill.
    Healing your past, releasing your future : discover the roots of your problems, experience healing and break through to your God-given destiny /
Catherine Cahill Fabiano, Frank P. Fabiano.
        p. cm.
    Includes bibliographical references (p.   ) and index.
    ISBN 978-0-8307-6209-5 (trade paper : alk. paper)
    1. Faith development. 2. Developmental psychology. I. Fabiano, Frank P. II.
Title.
BV4637.F23 2012
248.8'6—dc23   2011045657

Dedication

To Father God, Jesus and the Holy Spirit . . .
who made this book possible.

In loving honor of
Frank . . .
my dearest love, best friend and true son of the Father.

Catherine

CONTENTS

ACKNOWLEDGMENTS

Healing Your Past, Releasing Your Future is born out of many years of prayer ministry to those wounded on their journey through life. We can never find the words to fully express our thankfulness to the Lord for the wisdom and understanding He has revealed to us so that He might heal and restore our own souls as well as the souls of countless others. We are in awe of the desire of the Lord to heal even the most wounded among us and restore our eternal destiny in His kingdom. Lord, we are eternally grateful.

This entire project has been an experience of God's grace from start to finish. Many people have come alongside us to offer prayer support, encouragement and practical help.

We send our special thanks to our grown children, Chris and Todd, and to our families, who have loved and inspired us over the years.

We are thankful to so many friends who have stood with us through these years. To those named and unnamed, we thank you with all of our hearts.

The prayers of many have sustained us, but there is one who has been our anchor in the spirit: Anne Marie Carlier. This project was born in prayer and sustained by prayer. Its success is, in large part, the fruit of her faithful intercession and the exact spiritual insights we needed at the perfect moment. We could not have done it without you. To Corrina Broulliard, our longstanding prayer warrior, who has also "labored in the spirit" to see this project birthed. Corrina has been our research assistant and has found hidden treasures on the Internet that have been invaluable in this project . . . many thanks.

To all of our YWAM family in every corner of the world, you all have been a source of inspiration and insight from the Lord. Thanks . . . Danke . . . Gracias . . . Dank . . . Merci . . . etc. . . .

Our deep and abiding thanks to John and Paula Sandford, who have pioneered in the revelation of healing hearts and souls with the Lord and have inspired us and personally heartened us to see this project birthed.

A very special thanks to Jackie Pullinger, our dear friend and one of our strongest advocates, who personally recommended the publishing of this work.

Regal Publishing, your faith in and commitment to the project have made it a reality, and for this opportunity we are most grateful. You have made it possible for us to fulfill our mandate from the Lord. A special thanks to Kim Bangs, our editor and project manager, who has become a dear friend and prayer partner through this venture to publication.

Last but not least, we want to thank all those who have opened their hearts to receive the ministry and have encouraged us to write the book. Without you, there would be no ministry . . . and no book.

FOREWORD

The first six years of life are the "incarnating" years. We are not speaking of physical incarnation. A person's spirit resonates in every cell of his or her body, from conception to death. But sometimes people do not motivationally accept being who they are as spirit, soul and body, thus failing to incarnate fully into who they are meant to become. Traumas and our reactions may cause us to withdraw or rebel. When either happens, we bury a portion of who we are, until eventually, having failed to incarnate, we lose even what we think we have (see Luke 19:24).

Even among born-anew Christians, many have persisted in thinking that the past is the past and has no effect on them. Unfortunately, too many people resist becoming aware that they have carried their *childish* reactions and coping mechanisms into the present, refusing to acknowledge these afflict and inhibit their present relationships and activities. Some Christians especially do this, claiming that their conversion ended the process of healing when in fact it only began it.

Frank and Catherine Fabiano do a good job of cataloging how each developmental period of a person's life, from womb to adulthood, becomes and remains a critical influence in all he or she thinks and does as an adult. Psychologists have shown us how nurture or the lack of it, in our infancy, blesses or cripples us emotionally and affects character development. The Fabianos reveal how our spiritual life is not something apart from, and having little to do with, all that psychology has revealed, but that we are one being, developing spiritually, emotionally and in every other way together. They show us how failure to develop happens because we do not "incarnate" properly.

But they don't leave us there, as though we could be saved by right knowledge if we just understood how we were formed—or malformed, as the case may be. They know that "you will know the truth, and the truth will set you free" (John 8:32) means more than mere head knowledge. It means to know Jesus, and He shall set you free. Throughout this book, diagnosis is intertwined beautifully with resolution—redemptive, healing love in our Lord Jesus Christ.

Too often in the past, psychology and Christianity have appeared to be antagonistic toward one another. Christians have reacted to what seems to them as determinism, as though psychology is saying that culture and society condition us, which of course does away with guilt (the necessary and blessed steppingstone to freedom in Christ). Whereas, Christians say that we have a personal spirit by which we choose how we will react to what forms us; thus guilt leads to freedom in Christ (who did not come to save the righteous but the guilty). Psychologists have often felt that Christians load people with guilt (for many psychologists, guilt is the *enemy* to freedom, since secular psychologists don't know Christ) and that Christians inhibit development of who we are through restrictive laws and fear.

The field of healing has greatly needed works that disparage neither side and show how psychological understanding and faith can work together to bring about healing and the full development of the Christlike character that God intends all of us to possess. In *Healing Your Past, Releasing Your Future*, the Fabianos dance us joyfully beyond the warfare of history into harmony and saving action. They show us psychologically how we are created to be developed, stage by stage, and how wounding inhibits or prevents that altogether; and then how the merciful ministry of the Lord Jesus Christ is to be employed, not only to set us free but to transform harmful events and their results into the blessing of a strong and helpful character.

Look to enjoy as you read. This is not a dry tome of arcane knowledge. It is a lively testimony that employs real stories of real lives to move its revelations beyond the too analytical left brain into the right brain of revelation and emotion. Freedom to breathe and enjoy life should result from your study of its pages. If that isn't what happens to you, read it again, only this time with a light heart and a hope of freedom. That is the Fabianos' hope for you—and beyond theirs, our Lord's.

John Sandford
Co-founder with Paula of Elijah House: Healing Hearts . . . Transforming Lives
Renowned Christian Author

INTRODUCTION

Maturity does not happen in a "microwave moment," nor is it an endowment bestowed on a person by virtue of growing older. Maturity is the quest of a lifetime. It is not a destination, but rather a purposeful and deliberate journey, a process of transformation. It will not happen automatically with the accumulation of years but rather requires a conscious act of submitting our will to the will of God working in us. Many of us have heard people say, "Maturity comes with age," but that is not true. "Old" comes with age. We can grow "old in the Lord" yet lack maturity. The mandate to mature is the highest calling for those who belong to Christ.

> It was he [Christ] who gave some to be apostles, some to be prophets, some to be evangelists, and some to be pastors and teachers, to prepare God's people for works of service, so that the body of Christ may be built up until we all reach unity in the faith and in the knowledge of the Son of God and become *mature, attaining to the whole measure of the fullness of Christ* (Eph. 4:11-13, emphasis added).

When we consider the standard of biblical maturity, none of us is completely mature. Yet, we are challenged to pursue maturity, to be transformed into the image of Christ, to open ourselves to the process of sanctification.

> Instead, speaking the truth in love, we will in all things *grow up* into him who is the Head, that is, Christ (Eph. 4:15, emphasis added).

Hindrances to Maturity

The shortcomings of our natural human development affect our maturing process in the Lord.

The spiritual did not come first, but the natural, and after that the spiritual (1 Cor. 15:46).

Just as we need to be "born again" (John 3:7), so also we need to "grow up" again to become all that the Father created us to be.

Like newborn babies, crave pure spiritual milk, so that by it you may *grow up* in your salvation, now that you have tasted that the Lord is good (1 Pet. 2:2-3, emphasis added).[1]

Our past is ever present. The whole of our life is influenced by what has gone before. We can no more detach the present from the past than a tree can walk away from its roots. To move forward on our quest to maturity requires three things:

1. We must understand the process of human development as God intended it to be;

2. We must recognize how the "roots" of our adult problems were planted in our infancy and childhood;

3. We must experience the healing and restoration of the Lord as we relive the events of the past in His revealed presence.

Jesus made provision for all of our needs through salvation. In the original Greek, the word *sozo,* meaning "to save" or "to be saved," also denotes healing, health, wholeness, deliverance, well-being, safety, soundness and eternal life (see Matt. 9:22; Mark 3:4; Luke 8:36). Jesus also indicated in Luke 4:18 that His messianic ministry would include binding up the brokenhearted (see also Isa. 61:1). In 3 John 1:2, the apostle John prays that Gaius may be whole in body and soul: "I pray that you may enjoy good health and that all may go well with you, even as your soul is getting along well." This suggests that the Lord wants us to be whole in body and in soul so that we can prosper in His calling on each of our lives. As Christians, we often overemphasize eternal life and neglect to lay hold of the healing and deliverance we need in this life. One practical benefit of salvation is experiencing the healing the Lord provides to restore us to wholeness.

God's Plan for Human Development

Father God has a plan for human development. Unfortunately, we human beings have not understood it. For generations we have leaned on our own understanding (see Prov. 3:5) and, as a result, have made grave errors that have caused serious deficits and wounding to generations of God's children, including ourselves. Many of us, troubled by our failures in life, wonder why we are the way we are. The truth is that we have unmet needs and emotional wounds from our early years, which have a lingering impact on our lives. Father God knows each one of us intimately and understands our needs. He is the answer to every heart cry. He longs to heal us and redeem all that has been lost. Whatever wounds we have suffered or inflicted upon others, Father God will have the last word: "He sent forth his word and healed them" (Ps. 107:20).

Weeds and Roots

And some [seed] fell among thorns, and the thorns sprang up and choked them (Matt. 13:7, *NKJV*).

Now he who received seed among the thorns is he who hears the word, and the *cares of this world* and the deceitfulness of riches choke the word, and he becomes unfruitful (Matt. 13:22, *NKJV*, emphasis added).

The parable of the seeds shows how God sows the good seeds of His Word in our hearts and lives (see Matt. 13:3-23, where the field represents the heart of a person). Likewise, Satan can also sow bad seeds wherever God has sown good seeds, as Jesus indicated in a similar parable (see Matt. 13:27-28). There are two ways in which our experiences in early life hinder us from becoming mature. The first is through unmet developmental needs. If, in infancy and childhood, some of our needs remained unmet, we entered adulthood lacking some of the resources we needed to become mature people. We cannot give what we have not received. Our neediness not only hinders us, but it also impoverishes our capacity to give to the next generation.

The second way in which we are inhibited in our maturation process is by the wounds inflicted on us by parents, caretakers and other people who had a formative influence in our early life. These negative influences sown as seeds in our early months and years of life come to harvest in our adult life as fears, pain, shame, insecurities, sin and cyclical problems. The wound causes a lie to be planted into our hearts, perverting our belief system. This harvest has a debilitating effect, frustrating us and often tripping us up in our quest for maturity. We get stuck and find ourselves confronting the same issues over and over again. This continues until we get to the root cause. The Lord promises to rid us of these "roots" in our lives.

In Matthew 15:13, Jesus said, "Every plant that my heavenly Father has not planted will be pulled up by the roots." Although Jesus was speaking to the Pharisees, the principle is clearly not restricted to them alone. In Jude 1:12, we read that false teachers and leaders will be uprooted from among God's people, so the general principle stands that the Lord will uproot every bad seed and plant that has been planted by Satan in the hearts of God's people.

How Healing Can Happen

An unidentified commentator once observed, "The past is not the past: it lives on in memory." Psychological and neurological studies of the brain have revealed that everything that has ever happened to us in our life remains a part of us. In 1951, Dr. Wilder Penfield, a neurosurgeon at McGill University, made a startling discovery. He found that if he stimulated the temporal cortex of the brain (the frontal lobe of each side of the brain near the temple) with an electrical stimulation during surgery, the patient would vividly recall a specific past event and experience it as if it were happening in the present moment, with all the feelings that occurred when the original experience happened. Dr Penfield reported:

> The subject feels again the emotion which the situation originally produced in him, and he is aware of the same interpretations, true or false, which he himself gave to the experience in the first place. This evoked recollection is not the exact photographic or phonographic reproduction of past scenes or events. It is a reproduction of what the patient saw and heard, felt and understood.[2]

He further demonstrated that a person could occupy two aspects of conscious awareness simultaneously. In one case, he described the patient crying out that he heard people laughing. The patient somehow had double consciousness of two simultaneous situations—one in the present, and the other forced into his conscious awareness from the past, by electrical stimulation. Dr. Penfield writes, "When such a memory is forced into a patient's consciousness, it seems to him to be a present experience. Only when it is over does he recognize it is a vivid memory of the past. Such a memory is as clear as it would have been thirty seconds after the original experience."[3]

Penfield, Jasper and Roberts emphasize the difference between the re-experiencing of such complete memories and the isolated phenomena that occur on stimulation of the visual or auditory cortex or the memory for speech and words. They stress that the temporal recording carries with it important psychical elements, such as an understanding of the meaning of the experience and the emotion it may have aroused.[4]

Generally speaking, when the temporal cortex at either side of the brain is stimulated by electrical charge, the evoked memory becomes as imminent and vivid as the present. What is brought to life is a personal reliving of a specific experience.

In times of healing prayer, we have witnessed and personally experienced the Holy Spirit "stimulate" memory, although in a much less intrusive manner than that carried out by Penfield. A person touched by the Holy Spirit in this way re-experiences in the present an actual event of the past. He or she is aware of the true present and yet is simultaneously fully immersed in the living memory. The origin, or root cause, of an adult problem is brought to light, but it does not end there. The Lord reveals His presence in the memory of the person who is receiving healing and changes the images of the past and their effect. His presence renews and transforms everything. The old images give way to the new experience of Jesus—our Healer, Protector and Savior—reliving that time with us.

KAREN'S STORY

Karen kept watch through a crack in her bedroom door. Her father was an alcoholic and would often erupt in violent drunken rages. She feared for her mother's safety, so she kept vigil, naively believing that if things got out of hand, she could save her.

Karen had all but forgotten that experience when, in a time of healing prayer, the Holy Spirit brought it back with vivid clarity. This time she asked the Lord to reveal His presence there. Suddenly, in her memory, as she kept her vigil, the door opened— and there stood Jesus. He reached down, took her into His arms and carried her to her bed. As He tucked her in, He comforted her and reassured her. She could not save her mom, but He could. He walked out the door and closed it, and as Karen closed her eyes to sleep, she heard something amazing . . . it was quiet.

That night the Lord lifted an immense burden from Karen's heart. Now, whenever she remembers that time of keeping vigil when she was a child, she never "sees" it the old way: she "sees" the new version. Jesus is there, and His presence changes everything.

Father God's Intervention

God is ever present, even though we are not always aware of it. He was there at the beginning of our life, during our infancy, as we learned to walk, through our childhood and teen years; and He is here today. He is ever present, watching over our lives.

It was I who taught Ephraim to walk, taking them by the arms; *but they did not realize it was I who healed them. I led them with cords of human kindness, with ties of love; I lifted the yoke from their neck and bent down to feed them* (Hos. 11:3-4, emphasis added).

In the light of this truth, the inevitable question is, "If God was really there, why did He allow bad things to happen to me?" It's a fair question that deserves an honest answer. The short answer is, free will. When He created us, God gave us free will, and He will not take it back. Free will is what makes us unique, created in His image and likeness, and it sets us apart in all of God's creation. The choices of our parents, caretakers and other authority figures determined the good or evil that befell us. Wherever there is sin, someone gets hurt. Father God knew this would happen, and so He planned a way of redemption.

Our fathers disciplined us for a little while as they thought best; but God disciplines us for our good, that we may share in his holiness (Heb. 12:10).

Discipline in this context means to teach, train, nurture, correct, and so on. The problem here is that our fathers did "what they thought best" rather than what God's Word said was best. God makes a clear differentiation between our ways and His ways:

As the heavens are higher than the earth, so are my ways higher than your ways and my thoughts than your thoughts (Isa. 55:9).

In Hebrews 12:10, there is a little hinge that swings a mighty door—the word "but." This word functions like an eraser to wipe out all that went before and establishes what comes after. This understanding helps us to hear what Father God is saying to us. In an updated paraphrase, it might read, "Yes, yes, I know what happened. Your fathers did the best they knew how; but I am going to take care of all that. I am going to 'father' you again. I am going to teach you, train you, correct you, nurture you, provide for all your needs, for your good, that you may share in My holiness."

The Father wants to restore us because He loves us and wants us to share in His holiness. He wants us to be pure, blameless and holy. If we are to be all that God intended for us to be, we need Him to do a supernatural work in our lives. We were born to a destiny that can only be fulfilled as the Father redeems and restores us to be all that He created us to be in the first place.

Bryan Jones, a respected man of God from England, was speaking at a pastors' conference in Tucson, Arizona, some years ago and shared this story. Bryan and his wife take delight in buying and restoring old English cottages to their original beauty. One day, as he was working on a piece of antique furniture, the Lord said to him, "Bryan, how do you restore furniture to its original condition?" Bryan explained the step-by-step process of restoration to the Lord, as if He didn't know. The Lord then responded, "When I restore My children, I don't restore them to their original condition: I restore them to *My original intention*."

Father God's Healing Process

> The Lord's desire is that we bear fruit and fulfill His destiny for our lives. This is possible only if we become desperate enough to stop covering up our fears, pains, insecurities and sin and allow Him to replace our compensatory facades with His healing virtue and power.[5]

It's true. The Father loves each of us. He loves us with an everlasting love, without any conditions. He loves us in our pain, our immaturity, our neediness. But He loves us all too much to leave us there. The Father knows the frailty of our human flesh; He knows that we are not perfect. He also knew that we would be wounded in this life. So, in His great love, He has prepared a way to redeem what was lost to us; He has prepared a way for us to be healed and set free from bondages, a way for us to be restored to *His original intention*.

Truth: Facing the Pain

To be free, we must be willing to look at the truth the Lord reveals to us.

> Go to the place of your greatest fear, and there you will find your greatest strength.[6]

All of us have been wounded in our emotional development. Our parents—even wonderful, loving, Christian parents—were not perfect, and they were not always able to meet all of our needs. In many cases, they also suffered from emotional wounds and unmet needs. They could not give what they had not received. The Father wants to put an end to this inheritance of pain from generation to generation. But we must face the truth as the first step to freedom. Jesus said:

> If you hold to my teaching, you are really my disciples. Then you will know the truth, and the truth will set you free (John 8:31-32).

We all have a natural tendency to protect our family and those we love, sometimes to the extent of denying the truth. It is not always easy to do, but if we are willing, the Holy Spirit—the Spirit of truth—will reveal the truth to us. Denial is not loyalty; it is deception. We do no dishonor to our parents when we are willing to see the truth as the Lord reveals it to us. It is the only way to freedom. To begin, face the pain with Jesus. Acknowledge the hurts, the fears, the insecurities, the problems, the shame and the need in your life. As you work your way through this book, focusing on each stage of your development, the Lord will reveal what He intended for your life and begin a process of healing and restoration.

Revelation: Revisiting the Scene

The next step is to identify the specific adult problem in your life and ask the Holy Spirit to reveal the "root" of this pain or need. He may stimulate a memory, a picture, an impression, awareness or some other way of "knowing." Sometimes there is just a vague awareness that "something is there," that "something happened." The Lord knows each of us, and He makes known the root cause of our pain or need in the way that is best for us. Not everyone "sees" pictures, and it is not necessary to "see" a picture to be healed. Some memories are too painful to be seen in sharp focus, and the Lord shields us from anything that would be too much for us to endure. Ask the Lord to reveal His presence to you in the way that is best for you. Ask Him to show you what the Father intended for you in that experience.

The presence of the Lord changes things. Here is the way author and healing prayer leader Leanne Payne explains what happens: "In the Presence, listening, our souls are re-mythologized. The words and pictures that come from God replace the old negative, lying words and inner images that have their genesis in the world, the flesh and the devil—all that underlies our need for healing and salvation."[7]

Redemption: Healing and Deliverance

Often, we are not wounded by what actually happened, but by our "perception" of reality. As Jesus ministers to us, He removes the "sting of death" and gives us newness of life. The Lord heals the wound, sets us free from bondages and pulls down demonic strongholds. Jesus comes to reveal the Father to us in a very real way, revisiting that earlier experience with us to provide for our needs, to protect us, nurture us and restore us, supernaturally, to His original intention.

Restoration: The Planting of the Lord

Through the process of restoration, the Lord recalls to life what has been lost to us. He supernaturally "plants" in us what He intended for us from the beginning. Often what the Father plants in us is the exact opposite of what the enemy has sown into us through the wounds of the past. The Lord gives us "beauty instead of ashes, the oil of gladness instead of mourning, and a garment of praise instead of a spirit of despair." His purpose is that "they will be called oaks of righteousness, a planting of the LORD for the display of His splendor" (Isa. 61:3).

Recently, I was sharing this revelation during a time of ministry when suddenly, at the back of the room, a woman exploded in an agonizing wail. The depth of her grief and the piercing pitch of sound sent a shudder over me as I moved toward her. The Lord said, "Tell her to call My name . . . *Jesus.*" I did as the Lord directed, and in a desperate, mournful cry she screamed, "Jeeeesus . . . Jeeesus . . . Jesus . . ." A holy hush fell in the room, and the strong presence of the Lord quieted her. Then she began to laugh. The more she laughed, the more she was filled with joy. The more she laughed, the more others caught the joy, until we were all laughing, with tears running down our faces. As the Lord poured out His "oil of joy," sorrow and mourning fled away, and many received healing just by being in the presence of the Lord.

Reparenting: Father, "Father Me . . ."

The Father longs to provide for our unmet needs and "father" us again in a very *real* way. Healing and deliverance are only the beginning of the process. As we seek the Father day by day, He will continue to nurture us and provide the love, guidance, direction, correction and instruction we need to mature in our newness of life. We are "born again" to "grow up" again into the fullness of all God created us to be. Setting our hearts on things above, we begin a journey to maturity, led by the Holy Spirit, through a process of transformations by the renewing of our minds so that we will become more and more like Jesus.

> God wants to turn crisis to victory, barrenness to greatness in our lives. Regardless of our circumstances the Lord wants to satisfy the longing in our souls. Though we may seem barren with great odds stacked against us, He has placed His seed of greatness in every one of us who has called on His name.[8]

From the Father's Heart

Freedom and healing are Father God's gifts to us through His Son, Jesus. If you have never personally received the Father's free gift, please pray this simple prayer and invite Jesus into your life today and begin the most exciting adventure you will ever know:

> Jesus, thank You for coming to save me. Please forgive my sins. I receive the free gift of salvation You offer me. Jesus, come into my life and be my Lord and my Savior. Amen.

Welcome to the family of God!

1

IN THE BEGINNING

Life in the Womb

LAURA'S STORY

Darkness . . . deep darkness enveloped Laura. So alone . . . she longed for her mother. The loneliness closed around her. Laura kicked frantically to make her presence known. No response. An adrenaline rush shocked her. All around her a strange sound . . . the sound of pain . . . her mother crying. The words were imperceptible to the little one in the womb . . . but the impression etched deep in her heart. Her dad was gone. When Laura was born, she was told she was born face first . . . her face bruised and battered . . . she never understood . . . she was looking for her father.

The journey of a lifetime does not begin at the moment of birth, but long before in the "secret place," under the comforting rhythm of a mother's heartbeat.

My frame was not hidden from you when I was made in the secret place. When I was woven together in the depths of the earth (Ps. 139:15).

In the beginning, God had a plan and purpose for your life—a divine destiny. That may be hard for you to believe, given your present circumstances. Nevertheless, it is true—you were brought to life for an eternal purpose. If you are not in touch with that destiny and clear about your purpose, something has gone wrong.

Before I was born the LORD called me; from my birth he has made mention of my name (Isa. 49:1).

The Source of Adult Problems

Some of our most perplexing personality problems in adulthood are deeply rooted in our impressions from the womb. Yet these experiences—hidden from conscious awareness just beyond the grasp of cognitive recall in that gray space referred to as pre-memory impressions or memory traces—direct and influence some of our most fundamental emotional responses, thought processes and behavior patterns.[1] They are very real existential crises, yet just out of memory's reach.

LAURA'S STORY (CONTINUED)

Shortly before her birth, Laura's dad returned to his wife and daughter. He suffered from "post traumatic stress disorder" (PTSD) and could not cope with impending fatherhood. He broke down and ran. His return was a relief, but the damage of abandonment had been done.

All through her life Laura had struggled with intermittent anxiety attacks that came from "out of nowhere," for no apparent reason. She was plagued with a fear of abandonment and kept choosing men who did just that, validating the lie. When under extreme stress, she would often hear the "voice of death"—suicide—seducing her to give up on life.

Though she could admit it to no one, she felt very much alone most of the time, as if there was a glass wall between her and others, even between her and God. At other times, she wondered if she should exist at all. Laura had serious problems in her life, and she knew it. Years of therapy and counseling had made her very aware of every detail of her problems and trained her in excellent coping strategies to be able to manage them. But she wasn't free.

Laura's story is all too familiar. Long before we human beings are capable of cognitive thought, we are impacted and deeply impressed in our "being" by the atmosphere and influences of the womb. In a very real sense, what happens in the womb establishes the foundation for a person's life.

At this earliest stage of development, the very serious impressions we receive include: "I am to exist . . . I am not to exist . . . I do belong . . . I don't belong . . . I am accepted . . . I am rejected." Our experiences in the womb determine which of these impressions impact us the most and, subsequently, affect us in later life. If we did not receive what the Lord intended for our development, then we are hindered in our adult life.

These adult problems are often rooted in the womb experience: existence issues, rejection issues, anxiety disorders, "autistic" behaviors and insecurity in belonging or having a place in this world. Each of these adult behavioral indicators helps us identify which impression may have been prevalent in the womb. In other words, our adult problems highlight the wounds of the past and bring the specific need for healing into the light where it can be seen. Recognizing our need is the first step in the healing process. The adult behavioral manifestations can be summarized like this:

- *Existence* issues are struggles with life and death that range from ambivalence about life to suicidal thoughts and compulsions.

- *Rejection* may be actual, or it may be a denial of acceptance, care and love, which causes a person to feel worthless.

- *Anxiety* disorders range from chronic states of uneasiness, apprehension or restlessness, to sudden, intermittent panic attacks.

- *Autistic behaviors* hinder the ability to establish or maintain close emotional relationships with others.

- *Insecurity* affects stability in life. This gives rise to questions and struggles with being and belonging, which cause chronic uncertainty.

Pre-Birth Developmental Process

In order to grasp how these problems take hold of a person, it is important to understand the process of development in the womb.

For you created my inmost being; you knit me together in my mother's womb. I praise you because I am fearfully and wonderfully made; your works are wonderful, I know that full well. My frame was not hidden from you when I was made in the secret place. When I was woven together in the depths of the earth, your eyes saw my unformed body. All the days ordained for me were written in your book before one of them came to be (Ps. 139:13-16).

From the moment of conception, we begin growing in spirit, soul and body. Endowed as we are with an innate personality and eternal destiny, the process of development will either enhance or diminish the person we are becoming. This time of development sets the foundation for our whole life and is crucial to later development as well. No other stage of development so dramatically impacts the whole of our life. Acceptance or rejection, life or death, are the realities confronting us in the womb. The result of this time of development can be positive or negative, depending on what happens. A weak or faulty foundation affects stability in later life. Wherever the foundation is missing altogether, there is no platform on which to build.

New technology has made it possible to study the life of a child in the womb, and make some amazing discoveries. The child in the womb is very impressionable and far more alert and inter-active than had been realized before.[2]

Researchers now believe there is a degree of awareness even from the moment of conception.[3] The child is very sensitive to the atmosphere within the womb in the earliest weeks and months. In later months, particularly in the last trimester, the child can be directly affected by external sounds as well.[4] The Bible affirms this truth in a familiar passage.

> When Elizabeth heard Mary's greeting, the baby leaped in her womb, and Elizabeth was filled with the Holy Spirit. In a loud voice she exclaimed: "Blessed are you among women, and blessed is the child you will bear! . . . As soon as the sound of your greeting reached my ears, the baby in my womb leaped for joy" (Luke 1:41-42,44).

Initially, the most direct impact on the child comes from the mother, specifically the mother's thoughts and feelings.[5] How-ever, it is important to recognize that the mother's thoughts and feelings are most directly impacted by the father's thoughts and feelings toward her and the child.[6] So both parents play an im-portant part in the child's life from the earliest moments.

During a seminar a few years ago, a first-time expectant mother came up for prayer. Her due date was fast approaching, but the baby was in breach position.[7] The doctor had previously checked the baby and the mom, and everything was normal for natural birth. He had even turned the baby into position for birth, but overnight the baby moved back into breach position. As we prayed, the Holy Spirit revealed that the baby was in emo-tional distress. When we asked the woman if there had been any stress between her and her husband, she broke down in tears. Her husband had lost his job just after she became pregnant, and the financial stress was causing tremendous pressure on their marriage. They would often have violent arguments. The baby had been "listening" and was taking his "stand." He was not coming out.

Under the leading of the Holy Spirit, she placed her hand on her tummy and spoke to her baby. She told the little one what had been happening and assured the baby that they loved and wanted him, and the stress was not his fault. We continued in prayer and asked the Lord to remove the anxiety and release His peace to the baby. That night, her husband did the same. By the next morning, the baby had turned into position for birth on his own. He was born naturally a few days later—a joyful, peaceful baby. The Lord had healed him.

Bonding: The Vital Connection

Bonding with our mothers is critical for us in the womb. There is no more vital connection in this unfolding drama of life. Should this connection be missing or hindered in any way, the effects are dramatic. Bonding can be positive, negative or lacking, because it does not happen automatically.

Dr. Thomas Verny, a pioneer in research to understand the unborn child, observes, "intrauterine bonding does not happen automatically: Love for the child and understanding of one's own feelings are needed to make it work."[8]

Bonding was once believed to be initiated at birth, but research now indicates that it begins in the womb.[9] Bonding is achieved through a system of communication between mother and child.[10] According to Dr. Verny, "Bonding occurs through three separate communication channels . . . capable of carrying messages from baby to mother or from mother to baby." These three communications channels are *physiological, behavioral* and *sympathetic.*

Physiological Communication

The physiological connection with mom is essential and provides not only nourishment, but also transmits messages. If mom takes care to follow a healthy diet to provide everything needed for the baby to grow and develop properly, she sends a strong message: "Live, thrive, I love you, I want you to have all that you need to grow strong and healthy, and I will make sure you get it." It communicates a message of life, love and acceptance.

Behavioral Communication

The behavioral communication between mother and baby, and vice versa, is familiar and well documented. The baby kicks to communicate his or her need for attention, comfort or when in distress. When mom responds by rubbing her tummy and speaking to the baby in reassuring, comforting tones, mom and baby connect, and the emotional bond between them is strengthened. This maternal response affirms the baby's existence and provides the needed nurturing for the baby. Studies have found that the baby will kick when startled by loud noises and even to reassure mom when she is concerned about the baby.

Sympathetic Communication

Sympathetic communication is the least familiar and least understood in modern Western cultures. It is an intuitive communication between mother and child that transcends physical and behavioral limitations and requires a willingness to trust our senses.[11] This sensitivity of the baby to the thoughts and feelings of the mom, and vice versa, goes beyond behavioral communication.

Dr. Verny observes, "Rationalization and mechanization of the kind that has spread across Europe and America over the past few centuries seems to have destroyed that trust. Nature's enigmas make us uncomfortable. If we cannot explain something we prefer to ignore it."[12] Mom just seems to "know" what is needed. This intuitive knowledge is manifested in the maternal sensitivity, "knowing" the thoughts and feelings of the baby; and the baby's sensitivity in "knowing" the mother's thoughts and feelings.

Dr. Emil Reinhold, an Austrian obstetrician, studied fetal reaction to maternal emotion. He demonstrated how the baby is an active participant in intrauterine bonding. For the study, he had several mothers in their third trimester lie down and be still for 20 to 30 minutes under ultrasound. The baby relaxed in this position and stopped moving. The realization that the baby was not moving could cause panic in the mother. Seconds later, sensing the mother's distress, the baby started kicking intensely to reassure mom, "I'm okay." The baby reacted sympathetically to the mother's distress.

Emotional bonding forged through the behavioral and sympathetic communication between the mother and baby is not automatic; it is dependent upon the mother's ability to respond to "communication" received from the child. Even in the womb babies are beginning to try to "reach out and touch someone." One clear mode of communication by the baby in the latter months is movement. When a baby moves in his or her mother's womb, and she responds by speaking to the baby, he or she emotionally bonds with mom.

Moms who respond to their babies connect and complete their babies' initial attempts to be recognized, comforted in their need and affirmed in their existence. Through movement, babies are saying, "Mom . . . Hey, Mom . . . I'm here . . . Do you know it? . . . Is it okay???" Or "Mom . . . what was that LOUD noise? I don't like it!!!" When mom responds, speaking to her baby in soothing, reassuring tones, she affirms her baby's existence. The baby is comforted and the emotional bond is complete.

To understand just a little of what this must be like from the child's perspective, let's consider an illustration: Let's say you are in your house, locked in a closet. All your friends come over and bring your favorite pizza, turn on the music and laugh and talk together, but you are locked in your closet. What would you do? Probably start pounding and kicking the door to get someone's attention so they will respond to your need—in this case, to get out and join the party. In a similar way, the child needs to get mom's attention; so he or she begins to move and kick. Mom's response to that movement affirms his or her existence. Mom's willingness to respond to the child and also to call dad's attention to the child's movement establishes and strengthens the bonding not only with mom, but with dad as well. It is possible for the *in utero* child to hear and respond to external sounds and stimuli in the last trimester.[13] So when the father speaks in loving tones and is attentive to the child, the child begins to bond with him as well, even before birth.[14]

The child in the womb has even been known to interact with older siblings.

Jenna, pregnant with her second child, Paul, was bathing her firstborn, Joseph. Joseph was just two years old. In the course of bathing, Joseph accidentally whacked his mom's tummy and also Paul's bottom. Paul, not happy about the intrusion, started kicking back. Jenna pulled maternal rank on them both: "Hold it, I'm not getting in the middle of this. Paul, you have to wait until you come out to fight with your brother!"

Considering the biblical view of human beings as spirit, soul and body, we believe that bonding through communication to the spirit of the baby is also essential to the healthy development of the whole person in the womb. As parents pray for the child and communicate the Scripture and prophetic words that God gives for the little one, the child's spirit is nurtured and strengthened even in the womb.[15] This bonding promotes the development of the child's spirit and builds a foundation for his or her spiritual destiny in God's plan.

When we receive what we need in the womb—physical nurture to grow and thrive, healthy bonding to establish a relationship with mom and dad, and spiritual sustenance to strengthen our eternal purpose and destiny—a firm foundation is established for our life. If we don't receive what we need, destruction takes root and destabilizes our development.

Weeds and Roots

There is nothing concealed that will not be disclosed, or hidden that will not be made known (Matt. 10:26).

The wounds inflicted in the womb have a dramatic effect even into adult life. Most of what we have learned about these wounds and the destruction that takes root as a result has been through revelation by the Holy Spirit in over 25 years of counseling and prayer ministry. We have seen the Lord faithfully heal and set His people free as we have received and acted on the revelation He has given us. Each of these interventions has been repeated countless times by us and others and always results in life-changing healing and freedom. We have received countless testimonies of healing received directly from the Lord as individuals have applied the principles in the healing process and gone to the Lord with open hearts. (The healing process will be discussed in detail at the end of the chapter.)

The Lord has been intimately involved with forming us in our mother's womb and so His revelation is the most reliable source of information. However, there has been significant confirming research in recent years that objectively supports what the Lord has revealed (see Bibliography).

Wounds at Conception

As early as conception, a person can be wounded in his or her being. We have found that insecurity and shame are wounds often rooted in the circumstances of conception—out of wedlock, through rape or incest, in an atmosphere of violence or perversion. All of these circumstances inflict deep wounds. Individuals conceived in such circumstances often wonder if they should exist at all; their right to life is seriously undermined. The problem is often magnified when their parents tell them they are an "accident," a "mistake," a "surprise" or "unplanned." The truth is, our natural parents don't have the power to give us life. They cannot give us a spirit. It is our eternal Father who holds the power of life. When the Father breathes His breath of life into us and forms our spirit within us, He says yes to our life, and only then do we become a living being.

The One who gives us life is our true eternal Father. The power of this truth is life-changing. If you have lived with the lie that you should not be here, know this: Your life is more significant than the circumstances of your conception. The Father knew you *before* you were conceived. You may wonder, *Why would God give life to one who was conceived in horrifying circumstances?* God loves you. You are precious to God. No negative natural event can change that. His intention was always to redeem your life and restore you to be who He created you to be.

The LORD God formed the man from the dust of the ground and breathed into his nostrils the breath of life, and the man became a living being (Gen. 2:7).

The Spirit of God has made me; the breath of the Almighty gives me life (Job 33:4).

And he is not served by human hands, as if he needed anything, because he himself gives all men life and breath and everything else (Acts 17:25).

The mother is often tormented by fear, guilt and shame and is under major stress in these cases. Whatever mom feels, the baby feels.[16] There is also an impression in the baby that says, "What mom feels is because of me," and so the baby takes on the shame. If you have been wounded in this way, you may struggle under a cloud of shame. You may not feel right about your existence or feel "driven" to earn the right to exist by performing to please others. Unconsciously, you are trying to earn your right to exist. You are trying to make up for your parents' choices, sin or shame and to carry their responsibility. Wounding at conception can leave an emotional scar that overshadows a person's entire life.

PAULA'S STORY

Paula was an overachiever, committed to every endeavor 180 percent, and a driven perfectionist. She ran at only two speeds, turbo or dead stop. The latter only when she could not physically keep going. She never felt like she could rest unless she was sick or exhausted. Even when flat on her back she felt guilty. Paula was a shining star, or maybe a better description would be a meteorite shooting brilliantly across the sky of life. She probably never would have noticed she had a problem until she physically collapsed and was not able to recover her strength. She came within a hairbreadth of chronic fatigue syndrome when the Lord finally got her attention.

In a desperate moment she asked the Lord what was happening. That was all He was waiting for.

Paula had been conceived before her parents were married. They were committed Christians, so the shame was very intense. Her mother suffered under a heavy burden of internal guilt, condemnation and shame. No one knew except Paula. She felt responsible for her mother's pain and tried to help her carry it. Paula had a strong impression that she needed to be a very special person to earn the right to live. She loved her mom and was especially protective of her. When the Lord revealed His presence, she saw for the first time that she was in chains. She was enslaved by her perceived expectations from her parents. Paula was also burdened by her mom's guilt and shame. Jesus lifted her burden and broke the chains of slavery. He breathed over her again the breath of life and she breathed deeply, as if for the first time. Once freed from the lies and bondages of the enemy, she was able to recover her strength and begin to learn to be led by the Spirit.

Sometimes the effect is different on the child.

AL'S STORY

Al was plagued by perverse thoughts and a deep sense of shame. He repented, fasted and prayed but could not break through. When he came for ministry we asked the Lord to reveal the root cause of this recurring oppression in his life. The Holy Spirit gave Al a picture of a tiny cluster of cells overshadowed by a dark cloud. The picture revealed the time of wounding, and the Holy Spirit led us to understand that Al had been conceived in violence and perversion. This had been imparted into his life at conception. Al confirmed that his parents had had a horrifyingly violent life together. Sexual perversion and addiction to hardcore pornography were prevalent in his family. Being conceived in violence, compounded by the generational curse of sexual perversion and addiction to pornography, as well as being overshadowed by the shame of his parents' violent sexuality, had had a devastating effect on Al's life.[17] Al asked the Lord to reveal His presence to him in that picture and show him what the Father intended for his life. He heard the Father call his name and sensed a freshness all around him and in him—the "breath of life." The grayness that surrounded him at conception dissipated as the Lord revealed His presence in that moment.

Al clearly saw the truth for the first time—he saw that the circumstances of his conception were *not* the will of God, but his life *was*. For God Himself, true to His word, had brought Al to life. Father God had breathed the breath of life into him and he had become a living being (see Gen. 2:7). Al's life was not a mistake of nature; his eternal Father planned his life. The Father claimed him and took Al into His hands, and suddenly the picture changed. Al saw himself coming to life in a burst of light, brilliant with color, in celebration and purity. From that moment on, he was free from the heavy oppression of perversion and shame and felt clean for the first time in his life. Al asked the Lord to forgive the perversion of his forefathers, and he forgave them. He was released from the inheritance of shame, perversion and addiction, and he received his inheritance of life through Christ, according to Galatians 3:13. In the days that followed, the enemy again tried to assault him with thoughts of perversion, but this time when Al resisted the enemy, he did flee from him. The stronghold had been broken and Al knew he was free. The truth had set him free.

Wounds in Bonding

The wounds that occur in the bonding process can cause serious destruction to take root in a person's life. These roots include insecurity, rejection, existence issues, "autistic" behaviors and anxiety disorders.

Insecurity in Existence

Insecurity in existence frequently comes from a mother's pervasive ambivalence about her pregnancy and, in effect, the baby's life.

This is not to say that every mother who has fleeting misgivings about an unexpected pregnancy has wounded her child. It is rather the impression imparted to the baby by an extended or continuous ambivalence or rejection.[18] A mother who is ambivalent about her pregnancy may send mixed messages to the baby. The message "I'm not sure I want you . . . sometimes I do and sometimes I don't" is unsettling for the baby. If this ambivalence is of long duration or is a consistent pattern throughout the pregnancy, the child becomes ambivalent about his or her own existence and belonging: "If mom is not too sure I should be here, I am not too sure I should be here." The child in the womb is so sensitive that even the subtle feelings of ambivalence in mom can leave an indelible impression on him or her.[19]

The ambivalent mix of messages can rob us of complete security in existence and certainty of belonging in this world. If you struggle with existence, if you are never able to fully engage life or if you don't even know what we are talking about, you may be existing on the surface of life. In that case, having a real impact in this world is very difficult, as is feeling grounded and secure.

MARY'S STORY

Mary was forever apologizing. It seemed she was sorry for everything, even if it was not her fault. Her insecurity made it difficult to be around her. Mary was the proverbial "wallflower," hanging on the edges of a group, never really joining in. It was impossible to do anything for her; she could not accept any care. She was skating on the surface of life and never really engaging it. Over the years she became more and more withdrawn until a good friend challenged her to ask the Lord what this behavior was about. When she did, He reminded her that she was a surprise to her parents, conceived in their later years. She felt she was a burden to them even in the womb and tried to be as little trouble as possible. She never felt she had a right to ask for her needs to be met. In fact, Mary never really received her "birthright." The Lord revealed that He gave her life; He planned for her life. He welcomed her to life, and she heard Him proclaim her birthright: "You are to live and not die, and proclaim the works of the Lord. You have a place; you do belong here." The truth broke the power of the lie. Mary was able to embrace her life—the life her eternal Father had given her. She received her birthright from her eternal Father. No longer would Mary just exist, just going through the motions of life. Now she could begin to really *live her life.*

Insecurity in existence sometimes is the result of life circumstances. Before the introduction of ultrasound and the modern technologies we have today, some children in the womb went undetected before birth. In the case of twins there have been incidents of the second child being a surprise at birth. Even though the parents were loving, accepting and nurturing of the child in the womb, they were focused on one—the firstborn. The second child, of whom they were unaware, felt abandoned and insecure.

MIKE AND MATT'S STORY

Mike and Matt are twin brothers. Mike, the firstborn, is confident, secure and successful in whatever he does in life. Matt, the second born, is just the opposite. He is insecure, fears abandonment, suffers from anxiety attacks and feels like there is an invisible wall between him and others. For years Matt suffered, not understanding why there was such a huge difference between him and his twin brother. During a seminar as we were teaching about abandonment in the womb, Matt felt an ache inside. This was speaking to him somehow. During ministry the Lord showed him that he had been hidden behind his brother in the womb; his parents had not known he existed. As he asked the Lord to reveal what the Father really wanted for that time of his life, he felt the Lord's presence and realized he was being cradled in the hands of Jesus. The tension of holding it all together on his own broke, and he released the pain of a lifetime in gut-wrenching sobs. Matt became visibly relaxed as the Lord held him and spoke the love and acceptance over him that he so desperately needed to hear.

Insecurity in Identity

Male/female identity is at the heart of who we are and is essential to our security as a person. The words "It's a boy" or "It's a girl" herald our birth. Insecurity in identity is a reaction that comes from an initial rejection of our intrinsic identity as a boy or a girl from one or both parents. If your parents wanted a boy, and you are a girl, or they wanted a girl, and you are a boy, the rejection can cause insecurity in the essence of being either a girl or a boy. Somehow we don't feel quite right, and no matter how much we may accomplish in life we never feel quite good enough. The experience of not being "good enough" or "not right" for our parents is seriously distressing. When our identity as a boy or girl is not right for our parents, insecurity destabilizes our true sense of who we are to be.

Rejection

Chronic rejection by others and toward others can have a debilitating effect on our relationships. Rejection is being denied acceptance, care, love and so on, and can cause a person to feel worthless. If you have known rejection "for as long as you can remember," then most likely it began in the womb. The child in the womb is aware of rejection in mom's thoughts and feelings and, in some cases, is aware of the father's rejection. Messages that say, "I don't want you . . . you're an inconvenience . . . you weren't planned . . . you're not welcome" rob a child of the security of acceptance and certainty of belonging. Children who are unwanted come to expect rejection, and over the years they build up defensive reactions and behaviors for self-protection. They will begin to reject others before others reject them. The related problem, fear of rejection, can complicate matters, causing individuals to give other people undue power over them in an attempt to avoid being rejected.

When parents reject our existence or our identity, we never feel right about ourselves. We can come under the influence of a "spirit of rejection" that makes sure rejection keeps coming, and we may begin to take on a victim position in life. Encountering the presence of the Lord in the womb changes distorted, lying perceptions and brings the truth to light. Once a person is set free from the "spirit of rejection," dramatic changes take place. Tormenting rejection and fear of rejection give way to the loving acceptance and favor of the Lord. The truth of Father God's love becomes real to us. His perfect love drives out all fear.

> Though my father and mother forsake me, the LORD will receive me (Ps. 27:10).

Existence Issues

Existence issues of a more severe nature are those associated with the oppression of death. We have encountered hundreds of people with this oppression, and in almost every case the oppression was rooted in the womb. This can happen in a number of ways. The most direct cause comes through abortion attempts against the child's life. A direct assault on the child's life gives the enemy permission to attack the child. If not successful in taking the life of the child in the womb, the "spirit of death" will continue to oppress the person, pushing or seducing him or her toward death.

Another way this oppression can come on a person's life is through "death wishes" and "curses" (see Prov. 26:2; 18:21; Rom. 12:14). If the mother or some other person speaks a curse or death wish over the child in the womb, again the enemy is given permission to latch on and attempt to fulfill the curse. It is especially strong if the mother or father releases the curse against their child.

BARBARA'S STORY

Barbara struggled to exist each day. Severely depressive, the desire to die was ever seducing her. Her waking moments were plagued with questions: "Why did God do this to me?" "Why do I have to live when most of life is so painful and disappointing?" Finally, wearied from this struggle, she was ready to deal with the root of the problem. In prayer she asked the Lord where this was coming from. Barbara sensed herself in the womb and she "heard" her father's voice screaming, "I wish you would die—both of you!" Those words were a curse on Barbara, opening the door to the oppression of death against her life. Barbara felt the darkness closing in on her. She cried to the Lord and immediately He was present with her, and she experienced the reality of His love surrounding her—His life shielding her from death. Barbara agreed with that life and told death to go, in Jesus' name. She knew that Father God loved her, that He wanted her. She felt a big YES planted in her heart, spoken over her life from her true Father, her eternal Father God. Now the troubling questions were gone and she had her answer. The depression was gone, the hopelessness was gone, the death was gone and the joy for life had come—a gift of life from her true Father. Now free, she was able to forgive her natural father and pray for the Lord to touch his life.

Cultic rituals or curses over a child in the womb can also open the way for demonic oppression. A family history of witchcraft, sorcery, divination or other false spirituality, such as Freemasonry, can be an open door for the oppression of death.

ERIKA'S STORY

Erika accepted Jesus as her Savior and Lord in her teen years. Before this time she had lived a fairly normal life. After her conversion she started experiencing bizarre nightmares—evil, dark beings chasing her, trying to kill her. She would cry out "JESUS" and then they would be gone, but dreams with similar themes came night after night. After years of torment, she came for prayer during a healing seminar. The Lord revealed that her life had been dedicated to serve false spirituality and Freemasonry by her grandfather even before she was born. A curse of death would come upon her if she did not serve Freemasonry. When Erika became a Christian, the curse kicked in. The enemy could not take her life outright as she was under the blood of Jesus; but he had legal right through the generational curse to torment her and punish her for committing her life to Christ. When this curse was exposed, Erika asked God to forgive her grandfather and her forefathers. She forgave them and recommitted her life to the Lord. In the name and authority of Jesus, she broke the dedication of her life to serve Freemasonry and false spirituality. The curse of death punishing her was broken. She never had another tormenting dream. The cross of Christ had set her free.

Open assaults are easy to discern; however, there are other more subtle ways in which the oppression of death gains access. If death has taken a baby in the womb through abortion or miscarriage, the spirit of death may continue to oppress later children conceived and born.

NIKKI'S STORY

All through her life Nikki had near brushes with death. Her life began in crisis. Taken from the womb by Cesarean section at eight months, a sudden hemorrhage nearly claimed her and her mother's lives. Serious illnesses and accidents punctuated her life and posed threats to her wellbeing. She often dreamed of dying young, and in her dreams everyone would be grieving her loss. Nikki had developed a romantic view of death that masked its oppression. Not until the generational curse of romanticizing tragedy was broken was she able to see her need. She had suffered a double hit: her mom's miscarriage of a child just before her birth and the attack of death against her own life. Death was unmasked and revealed for what it was: an evil attempt to rob her of her life. Truth revealed the lie, and she chose life. She chose the truth that set her free in Jesus.

Sometimes the child born *after* a child has died in the womb feels guilty that he or she is alive and the other child has died. Often the surviving child will try to carry the life of the dead child and live life for them both.

KARA'S STORY

Kara was 35 years old, totally exhausted, often sick and beginning to look half dead. She was desperate for the Lord to do something. As we asked the Lord to reveal the root cause, I had a clear picture of Kara carrying a boy on her back with his arms around her neck. When asked about it, she told me it felt like that to her. The boy was her brother who had died in the womb before she was conceived. Her mother never stopped grieving the loss of her son. Kara got the impression that this brother's life was more valuable than her own and she felt guilty that she was alive and he was dead. She was somehow trying to carry his life. Living for two people is exhausting work, and she had become so bonded to her dead brother that she had started to die a bit herself. The spirit of death was beginning to lure her into giving up on life. When the cause was clearly revealed, Kara needed to release her brother to the Lord and take authority over the spirit of death, breaking its grip on her life. It was time to be free to live her own life and realize that her life was a gift from God—a gift of great value.

People may be under the oppression of death and not even realize it because they have never known life without it. There are indicators in adult life that reveal this oppression. If there is an oppression of death in your life, you can look back over your life and see a pattern of near-death accidents or illnesses. Another indicator is an obsession with death—frequent thoughts of death or dying or repeated nightmares about death or dying. It is also common with this oppression to hear the "voice of death"—suicide—under severe stress. This may manifest either as a fleeting thought or dream or by a driving compulsion. Suicide can be active or passive. Active suicide is a conscious, premeditated attempt to take your own life by your own hands. Passive suicide is not caring if you live or die, which can cause you to be careless and lose your life through an avoidable accident. The voice of death can be seductive, deceiving, even "religious."

A young woman I was counseling had endured a very hard life over a period of years. She was once again facing the pain of losing a man she had been sure she was to marry. This was only the most recent in a lifelong series of abuses, heartaches and disappointments. In her brokenness she confessed she had had enough. "Life is too painful. I can't take any more. I just want to go home and be with the Lord." The only problem was that she would have to die to do it. The voice of death with a religious twist is the most dangerous deception. The enemy knows that if he can get us to agree with death, he has an opportunity to bring it to pass.

How people react to the oppression of death is based on their personalities. Some are unaware of it and how it affects them. Others try to beat death by challenging it. When they feel threatened, they challenge death by running into risky, life-threatening situations; every time they survive it gives them a rush. But no one can beat death by human strength. Even this reaction is an indication of bondage and oppression. There is only one way to deal with death—by enforcing the victory Jesus won on the cross.

> Since the children have flesh and blood, he too shared in their humanity so that by his death he might destroy him who holds the power of death—that is, the devil—and free those who all their lives were held in slavery by their fear of death (Heb. 2:14-15).

If you recognize the oppression of death in your life, remember that the Father can and wants to set you free. His Spirit of Life swallows up death. Once the enemy is exposed and his works are brought into the light, he has no power. He can only operate in darkness and hidden places. For those who belong to Father God through Jesus Christ there is the promise of freedom. What the Lord reveals, He heals.

Autism: The Bondage

Another wounding experience directly related to lack of emotional bonding in the womb is the bondage of "autism." This is not psychotic autism of a severe nature that often relates to neurological damage, but rather an arresting of the normal developmental process. In the natural process, a child grows from self-awareness to "other" awareness and from an exclusively internal focus to integration that includes an external focus. Communication in the womb works two ways: (1) child to mom, and (2) mom to child.[20] When the child reaches out to mom and she responds and connects, there is no problem. However, if the child reaches out repeatedly and there is no response, he or she is left with a sense of abandonment and isolation. In order to survive, the child will close up, pull inside and try to make it on his/her own.

For various reasons, many of us have experienced abandonment in the womb. Life circumstances beyond our control, the realities of life in a fallen world, our mother's inability to form an emotional bond—all these can hinder the bonding between mother and child. This happens when the child tries to "communicate" with mom and there is no response, no connection, and therefore no emotional bonding.

Some hindrances on the mother's part may include the lack of a strong emotional bond with her own mother; trauma that distracts her attention from the child in the womb; or "frozen feelings" in her own life due to past wounds. We cannot give what we ourselves have not received. Often a mother who has suffered a miscarriage does not bond with the baby conceived afterwards, in order to protect herself from the pain of loss again. This lack of bonding can be conscious or unconscious. So, in a very real sense, for any of these reasons, the child is abandoned in the womb, is left in isolation and fails to make the first critical emotional bond in life.

To survive, the child intuitively regresses to natural autism, closes up inside and decides to focus inward instead of outward. In so doing the child is locked into a bondage of autism that continues into adult life. Those who suffer in this bondage often feel like they are on the outside looking in, wanting to connect yet totally at a loss to know how. They never seem to feel as though they belong or have a place. They have not been welcomed to life through the affirmation of their existence in the womb. Establishing or maintaining emotional, or heart, relationships is very difficult because they don't have that foundation of emotional bonding.

Nothing is more painful to live with than the feeling of isolation and loneliness. It is perplexing and frustrating to be able to function on the surface—to have amiable acquaintances—and yet be totally unable to move into deeper levels of commitment and intimacy with those dear to us. This is the feeling of being alone in a crowd, or the panic that erupts inside when someone wants to get closer to us. Running away or sabotaging the relationship are not uncommon responses to escape the pressure.

Another related problem is the ability to initiate emotional relationships but not be able to maintain them over time. This often happens when a mom initially connected emotionally with her child but trauma, tragedy or grief drew her attention away and the connection was broken.

The bondage of autism can also occur when the child blocks the bonding in self-defense. In some cases a child retreats into himself/herself to escape a perverted bonding to mom. An emotionally needy mom who takes comfort from her child, in the womb, is *pulling* life from the child instead of *giving* life to him/her. The child will block the bonding to survive. The Lord longs to restore this bonding and provide a firm foundation to build deep heart relationships. He still sets the captives free.

PETER'S STORY

Peter could not let anyone get close to him. He had a wall all around him 10 feet thick. His perception was that everyone was out to "suck him dry." Even his wife and kids could not reach him. When crisis hit his life, an emotional breakdown followed.

Now he had no choice. He had to deal with this irrational fear. In desperation he asked the Lord to reveal the root. He saw a picture of himself in the womb, trying to pull out the cord connecting him to his mother. He felt life being pulled from him. His mother was very needy and he was the youngest child of five. She was drawing emotional comfort from him. He felt that if he stayed connected he would be sucked dry and would die. Jesus revealed His presence and took Peter in His arms, shielding him from the neediness of his mother. Jesus touched the cord and the flow of life reversed. The life of God flowed into him, the walls of autism crumbled and he fell into the arms of the Lord. He chose to give up his prison of autism and allow the Lord to bond with him and protect him. The foundation had been set. Now he is growing in emotional relationships and loving deeply from his heart, protected by the healthy boundaries the Lord has set for his protection.

Insecurity with Belonging

Belonging is very important. When you often feel that you are on the outside looking in, trying to find your place and never really settling anywhere, it is an indication that you are insecure in your sense of belonging. A sense of belonging is not automatic. It is the fruit of being accepted and welcomed to life. When you are not welcomed and affirmed in your existence, you can begin to feel like your life is an imposition on others and you don't belong here. The result is insecurity in your sense of belonging and inability to find where you fit in.

Anxiety and Panic Attacks

Anxiety disorders can vary from chronic states of panic to being uneasy, apprehensive or worried about what might happen. If you cannot remember a time when you did not feel this way, then usually the problem has its roots in the womb.[21] Panic attacks are sudden, intermittent, severe attacks of anxiety that occur for no apparent reason and can be quite disabling. The unpredictability of the attacks can significantly undermine confidence and security and give place to the ever-pervasive fear of not knowing when the next one will strike.

Chronic anxiety and panic attacks are often rooted in trying to "carry" our mom's feelings and feeling that we have to help her. It is the sympathetic connection between mother and child that can allow this to happen. When a mother is struggling emotionally or physically during pregnancy, the baby may try to help her by carrying her feelings. The child senses that he or she must do this in order to survive. If you experienced this in the womb, you may feel burdened by anxiety, fear, grief, shame; or you may have a sense that you have unfairly carried depression with you your whole life. In many cases it is because, literally, *you have*—since the womb. You feel that you can never resolve these oppressive feelings because they are not your feelings; they belong to your mom. To get free, it is important to release those feelings to the Lord and also hand over the care of your mom to Jesus. The way to freedom is to break this unhealthy bondage and give her to Jesus, along with her burdens. Then the Lord can restore a healthy relationship between you and your mom.

The New Scientific Frontier: Fetal Origins

In the past 10 years, there has been an explosion of research studying the impact of the prenatal months on a person's life. This new field is called "fetal origins" or "developmental origins." The research reveals a link between the nine months in the womb and adult physical and mental health.

Diseases such as cancer, heart disease, obesity, diabetes, depression, anxiety and schizophrenia may have their beginnings in the womb. There are compelling results that are causing more serious consideration of this scenario. With this new understanding, there are ways being discovered to provide a life-giving environment in the womb that will support the health of the child in later life.[22]

The Holy Spirit brought this understanding to the light in the 1970s and 80s through the ministry of John and Paula Sandford and others who pioneered the need for healing in the womb. Frank and I have also received revelation of the impact on the developing personality in the womb, before there was confirming science. Through healing prayer led by the Holy Spirit, we have seen dramatic results and breakthroughs in our own family, as well as in the lives of thousands of others in our traveling ministry over the past 25 years.

As Christians, it is a knowledge that can help us pray for our healing and the healing of our children with understanding. Knowledge is a well that the Holy Spirit can draw from to give us direction for effective healing prayer.

The Vanishing Twin Syndrome

The Vanishing Twin Syndrome (VTS) is one of the studies that revolutionized our understanding of the impact of twins on each other from as early as the womb. VTS occurs when a twin dies in the womb or is miscarried in the first trimester of pregnancy and the remaining tissue gets absorbed by the remaining twin, by the mother or by the placenta, thus "vanishing." With improved technology and the onset of first trimester ultrasound screening, we are beginning to realize the sizeable impact of VTS. Not all incidents of VTS are known, but the estimates are that one in eight pregnancies that begin as twins or multiples later become singleton pregnancies. What impact does this have on the surviving twin? If the twin is lost in the first trimester, there is no physical harm or danger to the surviving twin.[23] Yet twins are known to form a bond with each other that is as strong as the maternal bond, and the emotional impact can be significant. Negative effects we have witnessed in the surviving twin are guilt, grief, compulsive control or overprotectiveness, fear of sudden loss or abandonment, fear of death, longing for a twin, dreams about the twin, and carrying the life of the twin—living for both of them.

TED'S STORY

Ted struggled with an irrational fear that those he loved might one day disappear. When his wife or children were late coming home and did not call, he would begin to panic. He would explode in anger with them and escalate his tendency to possessiveness and control. The oppression became unbearable until he prayed to ask the Lord to show him the root cause. He saw himself in the womb with his twin. They were very aware of each other and connecting. There was a sense of peace and comfort. Suddenly, his twin was gone, vanished. A strong sense of panic, pain and confusion hit his heart. What happened? Where did he go? Ted asked Jesus to come to him and show him. Jesus revealed His presence, holding Ted's twin, and explained that it was time for his twin to come home. Jesus told Ted there was a plan for his life and he needed to stay, but he would see his twin again and they would have all eternity to enjoy each other. When he saw his twin alive with Jesus, Ted could let him go. Then Jesus held Ted in His other arm and touched his heart. A strong peace filled him. Ted and Jesus were in command of the fear, panic, fear of death and fear of sudden loss or abandonment. Ted felt a heaviness lift from him. Next time his wife was late, he did not even notice, because a supernatural peace was guarding his heart and mind.

The Dream

A young mother had a recurring nightmare of seeing her youngest child at the bottom of a pool. She dove in to get him, and as she pulled him to the surface, she lost her grip and he fell to the bottom again. She knew he was lost, and she would wake up crying.

As a result, she became compulsively overprotective and smothering with her youngest child. Finally, she cried out to God to help her understand the dream. As she prayed, the Lord brought her back to the womb and revealed that the child at the bottom of the pool was her twin brother who was miscarried in the womb. She saw him falling out of the womb and heard herself crying, "I am sorry . . . I am sorry . . . I can't help you."

She cried to Jesus, and suddenly she saw Jesus catch her baby brother in His arms and hold him close. Her twin was alive and laughing in the arms of Jesus. She realized he was not dead, he was with Jesus, and she would see him again one day. She was finally able to break the bonding and let him go. Jesus healed the wounds of her trauma and set her free from the grief and guilt. After prayer, the compulsion to overprotect her child was gone. Once free from the compulsion, she could learn to change her behavior and develop a healthy relationship with her son.

Father God's Intervention
LAURA'S STORY (CONTINUED)

Remember Laura, whose story began this chapter? The stress on Laura became unbearable. Something had to change. As she sought the Lord, He revealed the root cause of her pain. In a moment, Laura was projected in her memory to the time when she was in her mother's womb. The darkness, the smothering, the painful cries of her mother enveloped her. The grief etched deeply in her being resurfaced, but this time she was not alone. Jesus was there. Still, a "glass wall" separated Laura from connecting with the Lord's presence, and the prison of autism held her; so we began to pray. In desperation Laura cried to the Lord and immediately He turned to her, and the wall melted away as He came near. Jesus cradled her and protected her. The darkness of death evaporated; the fear and grief gave way. Laura was experiencing the truth. It was the Lord who held her fast and shielded her life. It was the "everlasting arms beneath her" that secured her life. Now in the presence of Perfect Love, all fear and anxiety were put away. Jesus revealed the Father's love and care for her and quieted her anxious heart. For the first time in her life, Laura felt the security of being "connected." The emotional bonding had been restored with the Lord and the abandonment and isolation plaguing her life were brought down. Jesus now was her protection. She took her stand, in Jesus' name, against the oppression of death, fear of abandonment and bondage of autism; and she released to the Lord the grief and anxiety she had carried for her mother, and she was set free. Laura agreed with the truth and embraced the life and birthright Jesus had given her. She was to live, and not die, and proclaim what the Lord had done (see Ps. 118:17). She had a place in her Father's kingdom; she did belong. The Lord revealed that, in her desperation, Laura's mother had spoken curses and death wishes over her life. Laura broke those curses and forgave her mother. Finally, she broke the power of shame and grief, and the Lord released her from the lie that she was responsible for her mother's pain and her father's abandonment. Peace, security, life and belonging came to Laura—the planting of the Lord in her life for the display of His splendor.

Who shall separate us from the love of Christ? Shall trouble or hardship or persecution or famine or nakedness or danger or sword? . . . No, in all these things we are more than conquerors through him who loved us (Rom. 8:35,37).

Truth: Facing the Pain

Consider the adult problems identified in this chapter. Do you recognize any of these problems in your thoughts, feelings or behavior? It is important to face the truth. Only by confronting the truth can you be healed and set free.

Revelation: Revisiting the Scene

The problems you have identified in your life did not start yesterday. What happens in the womb affects us deeply, and only the Holy Spirit can reveal what is hidden from that time. Ask the Holy Spirit to reveal the truth to you.

Redemption: Healing and Deliverance

The Father wants to heal you and restore you to His original intention for your life. Ask Jesus how the Father intended that time to be. The Lord will uproot the destruction that was planted. When we ask Him, He supernaturally ministers healing and sets us free from bondages and demonic oppression supernaturally.

Restoration: The Planting of the Lord

Ask the Lord to provide for your emotional needs that went unmet during your development in the womb. He is able to restore to you all that you need and will supernaturally plant what He intended for you from the beginning—life, acceptance, belonging.

Reparenting: Father God, "Father" Us

The Father, by His Spirit, will help you "work out your salvation." He will teach you day by day how to walk in His ways, the ways of life. Father God will set boundaries for your protection and discipline you for your good, and the Holy Spirit will be with you, always ministering the heart of the Father. He is our Teacher and our Counselor (see John 14:26). God's Word is God's way. If you proclaim His Word as the final authority in every circumstance, and live it out in your life, then you will be set free and stay free.

THE FATHER'S HEALING PROCESS:
STEPS TO HEALING, FREEDOM AND RESTORATION

Healing

1. Identify the adult problems—feelings, thoughts or behaviors—that apply to you from this stage of development. (See Tables 1A/1B: Healthy/Unhealthy Development.)

2. Ask the Holy Spirit to reveal the root cause of each problem, i.e., whatever happened to you in the womb that caused a wounding in your life and allowed the problem to take root. The Holy Spirit may reveal this to you in the form of a memory, a picture, an impression, a thought, an awareness or some other way of "knowing" (see Luke 8:17).

3. Ask Jesus to reveal His presence with you there. The presence of the Lord changes everything (see Ps. 31:14-16; Heb. 13:5-6,8).

4. Tell Jesus what you are feeling and thinking in this time, place or experience. Listen to His response (see Pss. 88:1; 91:14-16).

5. Ask Jesus to reveal what the Father intended for this time of your life. Jesus comes to show us the Father. Allow the Lord to minister to you; rest in Him and take time to receive what you need. He comes to care for your developmental needs, to heal you, to redeem all that was lost to you and to restore you to be all He created you to be (see Jer. 29:11; 17:14).

Freedom

6. In the name of Jesus, break the power of the lie planted in your heart from the wound, and ask the Father to uproot it. Embrace the truth that has the power to set you free, which is the Word of God. Proclaim the promises in God's Word that are His answer to your need (see Matt. 15:13; John 8:31-32; 2 Cor. 1:20).

7. Identify any patterns of sin, bondages or curses passed from generation to generation in your family. Break any generational curses, if necessary (see Appendix A: Generational Curses). Forgive your parents and all those who wounded you (see Matt. 6:14; Gal. 3:13-14).

8. Take authority in Jesus' name over any demonic oppression or influences in your life that the Lord has revealed. In the name of Jesus and His authority, command them to leave (see Luke 10:19; Jas. 4:7).

Restoration

9. Receive Father God as your eternal Father and receive your inheritance of life through Christ Jesus. Seek the Father each day and ask Him to father you (John 10:10; Heb. 12:10).

10. Ask the Holy Spirit to teach you how to walk in your newness of life. Commit to listen to and obey the Holy Spirit and begin to put God's Word into action in your life (John 14:26; 16:13-15; Phil. 2:12-13).

Table 1A: Healthy Development

Stage of Life	Significant Issues	Developmental Task (needed for healthy development)	Adult Manifestation
In utero	Existence: to be/not to be	Bonding/connecting with mother	Secure in existence and life
	Acceptance/ rejection	Receive acceptance	Secure in belonging
	Belonging/ not belonging	Receive birthright	Secure in acceptance
		Embrace life	Secure in intrinsic identity
		Embrace intrinsic identity	Secure in Christ

Table 1B: Unhealthy Development

Stage of Life	Significant Issues	Developmental Task (needed for healthy development)	Adult Manifestation
In utero	Existence: to be/not to be	Needs ignored	Existence issues
		Existence discounted	Autistic behaviors
	Acceptance/ rejection	Treated with ambivalence or rejected	Rejection issues
	Belonging/ not belonging		Oppressed by death
		Lack of or insufficient bonding	Anxiety disorders Insecurity
		Abandoned	Panic attacks
		Abortion/ attempt or threat	Insecure in Christ
		Curses	

2

BEING

Birth to Six Months

Birth, for most of us, was the first trauma of life. Do you remember it?

For nine months—all my life—It has been so wonderful. Warm water cradles me in suspended peace. Mom's heartbeat comforts me and sometimes even excites me when it beats fast. I am upside down now. It is almost time to make my entry. It's getting a little cramped in here.

Suddenly, in an instant, swoosh—the water is gone.

Yuck! I'm vacuum-sealed! What is this sticky stuff? What's happening? I can feel pressure all around me. I'm being squeezed. The walls are closing in on me. This pressure is forcing me out. I'd better push, too, to get away from the squeezing. Oh no, I'm being squeezed through such a small opening, my head feels like it's going to be squished. PUSH!!! Here I come . . .

Wow, it's bright out here! Oh, where is Mom's heartbeat? Hold me, Mom . . . (sigh). Hey, what are they doing? Oh no! My lifeline! Not my lifeline . . . Don't cut my lifeline! WWWAAAAAAAAAAA!!!

Now what's happening?! I'm being wrapped up in something . . . They think this is soft? It's the itchiest thing I ever felt . . . WWWWAAAA !!!!

LIFE! How exciting, right? Hmm . . .

Each birth is a unique drama—mom and child working together to bring the little one into the world. God provides these first months of life to establish what it means to exist: our identity and self-image, our security in life and our feelings of basic trust. All these are essential in laying the foundations for effective thinking, problem solving and communication throughout life.

MARTHA'S STORY

Martha has difficulty speaking through her deep sobs. Finally, she is able to speak clearly as we sit and wait. "Suicide is my only option! So I tried to kill myself. God's love is not real for me. All my life I have been experiencing deep bouts of severe depression and an overwhelming sense of hopelessness."

When parents ignore God's way; when they impose their own needs, desires and expectations on a child; or when their care of the child is marred by their own infant wounds, demonstrated in reacting to his or her demands for care with confusion, frustration or selfishness, the results are devastating.

MARTHA'S STORY (CONTINUED)

My father and mother have always expected me to perform for them and be perfect in order to receive their love. This has been for as long as I can remember. I want to die, because I just can't strive any longer to reach this goal of expected perfection.

As a result of wounds suffered during the birth-to-six-month period, a person is likely to advance into the adult years believing, as Martha did, that it would be better not to exist at all. These wounds can cause people to feel insecure within themselves and insecure about their position in the world. If you have suffered in this way, then you may be overly dependent on others for care and may feel emotionally shut down, ignoring your feelings and the feelings of others. You may fall in and out of relationships, always experiencing the same disappointments. Your needs and expectations are never satisfied or, perhaps, never even attended to. You may also find that you regularly experience difficulty in thinking effectively and solving problems. Perhaps you find yourself being confronted by others because you missed the signals that a problem existed, and therefore failed to deal with it effectively. You may be the type of person who periodically explodes in uncontrollable anger when confronted with the conflicts and frustrations of life.

All of these real-life conditions, although prevalent in the general population, are not God's plan for you. They are symptomatic of major wounds that occurred very early in your life, during the time between birth and six months.

Developmental Process

A person's experiences during the period from birth through the first six months outside the womb build on the foundations of life that began at conception. A child's responsibilities appear to be simple—just to *be* and to receive nurture and care. However, closer scrutiny of this time reveals much about what is being incorporated into the child's life. Unconditional nurturing is required, as is care for all the child's needs. The child's survival depends on being fed, and even on being held and caressed, because in this way the body's life support systems and functions are stimulated.

Because human beings are spirit, soul and body, the primary needs for survival are spiritual, psychological and physiological. Father God intends for all three to be attended to by a newborn baby's caretakers in order to ensure that he or she grows and develops in the way He intended.

RALPH'S STORY

For 30 years, life for Ralph had been a burden. He found daily life to be very difficult, always a struggle, with nothing coming easy. Constant high levels of energy were required just to get by each day. During prayer, the Lord revealed something to Ralph that he had long since forgotten. Family conversations had frequently focused on how Ralph was finally born after his "poor mother went through a marathon labor." His mother had been in labor for over 12 hours, struggling, pushing and squeezing before Ralph finally came out. The long struggle to be born and the energy he expended in this process established a foundational pattern of life for Ralph. Just to live required him to expend a great deal of effort. The prayer time was dramatic for Ralph. The Lord brought him back to his birth. Jesus revealed Himself in the memory (see Ps. 22:9-10), calling Ralph forth, receiving him from his mother's womb and then receiving him into the world (see Ps. 71:6). I prayed, as the Lord encouraged Ralph to be born, that the Lord would make him easily delivered (see Exod. 1:19). At that moment, Ralph experienced an overwhelming sense of peace and security as he re-experienced his birth as the Lord had intended it to be. After this dramatic prayer time, Ralph perceived the normal conflicts and struggles of life much differently. Gone was the enormous energy drain just to make it through the day. No longer did life present itself as a never-ending series of burdensome struggles. Ralph was free to live life as God had originally intended for him.

The circumstances surrounding birth can set a pattern that influences the rest of life. Late births, premature births, cesarean births, instrument-assisted births all have their unique set of conditions and circumstances that are foundational and have a permanent influence throughout a person's life. They establish a foundation upon which the conditions of life are experienced and perceived. They can cause recurring patterns and struggles in life that prevent healthy growth and development to develop as God intended.

Survival and Existence

During our first six months of life, we are dependent on our primary needs being met for survival. We have *bodily*, or physiological, needs—for food, water, shelter, air, good hygiene. We have *soul*, or psychological, needs—for love, attention, being held and caressed. We have *spiritual* needs—for prayer, to have God's Word spoken to us, to have psalms and hymns sung to us. We use each of these areas of nurturing to identify what it means to exist outside the womb. The establishment of a sense of self-worth, belonging and affirmation is dependent on the quality of these experiences.

At this stage we learn about what internal and external existence means. Internal existence is self-concept learning. It is learning about our physiological, psychological and spiritual condition. For instance, we learn by being fed and the ensuing digestive process. If all is well, we experience a sense of wellbeing and establish a healthy self-perception. This is an elemental building block to forming a good self-image.

External existence is learning about everything in the outside world. We discover that we have arms, legs and feet, and we learn what the world is like. We find out if it is a good place or a hostile place. We learn this primarily by being held, touched and caressed. This sets the foundation to later understanding and distinguishing the boundaries between self and others. Being prayed over; having God's Word spoken to us; and having songs, psalms and hymns sung to us nourish our spirits and set the foundation upon which we can later develop and mature into a close interactive relationship with Father God.

The Symbiotic Relationship

The key to healthy development is the symbiotic relationship between mother and child.[1]

"Symbiosis" is a biological term. Basically, it refers to an interdependency in which two dissimilar organisms live together in a mutually beneficial relationship. Within this relationship there is a merging and sharing of needs. The mother has maternal instincts and needs to provide nurturing for the infant. The infant needs to receive that nurturing. Thus, in a healthy and normal relationship, the needs of both mother and infant are satisfied.

The mother experiences joy and fulfillment in nurturing her baby; the baby experiences this nurturing as encouragement to survive, grow and be healthy. A strong foundation of basic trust is now being established. Symbiosis is the bonding necessary for the infant to survive. Thus, symbiosis ensures survival and must be maintained. As the child develops and matures, the need for the symbiosis breaks down to its final resolution when the child is two years old. We will discuss this resolution in a later chapter. For our purposes here, we will focus on the symbiotic bond between mother and infant.

When a new mother received what she needed from her own mother for healthy growth and development during her infancy, she has within her the necessary resources to provide what her baby needs for healthy development.

Symbiosis is our first introduction to relationship. God provides this relationship so that we can learn about trust, what it means to exist in this world, who we are, what life is like, and what it will take to survive. The quality of the care we receive within the symbiotic relationship imprints upon our life the significance and worth of our existence, both internally and externally (see 1 Thess. 5:23).

The Feeding Process

It appears that the basic building blocks for all future adult thinking and problem solving are established during this time of life.[2] A great deal of research on human thought and problem solving exists, and it is not our intention at all to seek to replace this research or propose a theory designed to refute these studies. Our intention is to consider the functional, social-interactive understanding of the impact we have found the feeding process to have on a child, and to consider the results such influences have on adult life. For our purposes, we will break down all adult problem solving into three basic components: *feeling, thinking, doing.*

When all three components are appropriate to the situation and are accurately focused on, problems can be solved and situations handled effectively. (When we speak of the *feeling* component here, we mean this in a much broader sense than emotions such as happiness, sadness, anger, fear, and so on. This feeling component in the *feel-think-do* process includes these emotions, but it also includes anything within our environment that activates the nervous system, signaling the need for attention and requiring a response.) The feeding process provides one of the basic building blocks for learning to problem solve. As infants, when we are hungry, we experience hunger pangs in the form of stomach contractions. These contractions cause pain. We cry to signal that we hurt and that we need help and care. Mom's job is to figure out what we need, in this case food, and meet this need. Our part is to suck and take in nourishment to stop the contractions so the pain will cease. Thus, the need for food has been satisfied.

We need to learn this connection between the discomfort of hunger pangs, crying and sucking during the first three months of life. As we experience this process a number of times, we make the appropriate connection to satisfying our need. We learn to solve our first and most life-threatening problem. When mom allows us to feel the hunger before feeding us, she helps us become fully aware of our feelings, which motivates us to perform an act that will resolve the problem. She has helped to put the foundation in place for us to develop effective thinking and problem solving.

These three aspects of the feeding process—hunger pangs, crying and sucking—are related to the three aspects of adult problem solving—feeling, thinking and doing. As we grow and mature, hunger pangs and our attention to them are transformed to a higher order. We develop an ability to recognize our feelings and do something effective about them. Crying transforms to a higher order called thinking. We can still cry about our problems, but hopefully this does not remain our primary response to them. Thinking replaces crying as the method of dealing with life's issues. Sucking is an action. We learn that we are able to perform an act that will be effective in dealing with the issues of life.

Why Crying?

Father God gives all children a gift at birth. That gift is called *crying*. We believe that all parents desire to reinforce and affirm the gifts given to their children by God, and no matter what they may think about it, crying is not something meant to torment them. Crying is the foundation for learning how to communicate in this world.

All mothers agree that babies have different cries for different needs. Crying signals to mom that her baby needs food or comfort or a diaper change or help with an emergency ("My head's stuck in my crib"). When mom accurately discerns her baby's cry and responds appropriately to the need, baby learns that he/she is loved and cared for. That is how our existence is affirmed. We learn that it is okay to have needs and get those needs met. This is our first experience of unconditional love.

Through this experience we learn about effectively communicating our needs in this world. If mom does not respond in an appropriate way to the cry—acts in a way that increases our discomfort, resulting in more crying—we learn the opposite. We incorporate the belief that we do not belong in this world and should not exist. Later in this chapter we will explore in detail some problems that manifest in adult life when infant cries were handled inappropriately. Others' responses to our crying signals tell us whether we are encouraged to be here—to exist and be real.

Parents Count

Among all the things that parents need to do for their child at this time of life, one thing is imperative. Parents must take special care of their own needs for nurturing and being cared for so they can provide the best possible environment for themselves as well as for the child. This includes being healed of their own wounded past. Parents have a wonderful opportunity when their baby is this age to rethink, feel and experience their own being and dependency needs. Parents, like children, have developmental issues to work through. These issues will resurface to be dealt with at each developmental stage you go through with your children. If, as parents, you do not allow the Lord to heal you of your childhood wounds, you could wound your own children in the same way and at the same ages that you were wounded when you were a child.

The Significance of Father

So far we have focused on the mother as the major care provider. Yet, it is important to add that our natural father provides us with the first representation of Father God. We begin incorporating who Father God is as our own father relates and interacts with us and cares for us during this time of our development.

A study was conducted on the amount of time fathers spent per day verbally interacting with their infants from birth to three months old. The study found that, on average, fathers spent 37 seconds per day verbally relating to their infant.[3] Think about the impression the developing baby receives about Father God! If our early experience was like that, then we could grow into adulthood thinking that Father God does not have much time for us. Hence, we pray quickly and relate to God for short periods of time because, after all, God has only 37 seconds for us. He's too busy fighting famine, averting wars and alleviating poverty.

This may be an overreaction to the 37-second finding in the study, but it certainly drives home a point. Fathers need to spend much more time with their infants. Fathers provide a sense of security, protection and identity. Without the father's input, much of these very significant aspects of life are, at the very least, weak in the child's developing personality.

AGNES'S STORY

Now a young woman, Agnes reports, "All my life I have had problems with my father. We had no relationship from the day I was born. There was no physical contact and no verbal interaction with him. He didn't even discipline me. I grew up thinking men were useless, helpless and wimps. I did not feel capable of communicating my needs to them. Actually, I saw men as needing someone to care for them, because they weren't capable of taking care of themselves. I was strongly motivated to take care of men. Yet, I feared getting involved and hated them at the same time."

We will return to Agnes's story in the section "Crying Requires Response."

Weeds and Roots

In this section, we will consider each of the most important areas previously mentioned and point out what can happen in adult life when the infant is wounded at this age or not provided for as God intended.

Birth

The circumstances surrounding your birth can set patterns that continue to influence you through your life. Patterns from birth often affect any "new beginning" in life.

Premature Birth

Premature birth can cause you to never completely feel ready for new challenges in life. You may perceive the normal demands of life as being thrust upon you before you feel prepared to deal with them.

Induced Labor

Induced labor can result in growing up feeling pushed into new situations or circumstances of life that you do not feel ready to handle. You may even say the phrase, "Don't push me!"

Late Birth

Late birth can result in feeling as though you always seem to miss the opportunity to act or get involved in a timely manner, perceiving yourself as "too late."

Cesarean Birth

The cesarean-born infant may not struggle in the birth process because you are taken before the struggle. When confronted with normal challenges of life, you may remain passive and complacent, not persevering to work through life's problems.

If the cesarean is the result of a decision made by the doctor and the mother, nine months before the baby's estimated due date, the baby is not given the freedom to come when ready; the birth is controlled by others. In later life, a person may feel controlled by others and never feel as though he/she is in control of his or her own life. In fact, they easily give up control of their lives to others.

When the cesarean procedure is necessitated by a threat to your life, you may experience apprehension and heightened levels of panic, fear or anxiety when confronted with the normal struggles, challenges and new beginnings of life.

Instrument-Assisted Births
Instrument-assisted birth involves forceps or other equipment to pull or suck the baby out of the womb. It may be necessary if the baby is in crisis or not coming out for some reason. From this experience a person may resist anyone "pulling him" into situations he has not decided on for himself. He digs in his heals and refuses even reasonable suggestions.

Traumatic Birth
Life-threatening birth experience often results in panic, fear or anxiety erupting later in life whenever one is confronted with new beginnings. Outbursts of rage are also possible, linked to survival.

The First Six Months

Internal Existence
Babies who experience feeding problems, such as allergies to food, or digestive problems, such as colic, experience a deteriorating self-image. They begin to incorporate an unhealthy self-perception, which is then elemental to the formation of a poor self-image. People to whom we have ministered over the years who had colic or digestive problems as an infant describe themselves as insecure and have a tendency not to feel good about themselves.

Symbiotic Wounds
As already mentioned, symbiosis is the most impressionable relationship in our lives. It sets the pattern for all future relationships throughout life. When our needs at birth to six months are not appropriately attended to by our mother, we continue throughout

our entire life to seek the satisfaction of those needs. However, because those needs are *infant needs,* they will go unmet. No one will be able to meet them because they cannot go back in time and take the mother's place. Yet, many people continue to work at getting these needs met in their adult relationships. This is why there are so many disappointments in relationships, so many struggles, so many conflicts. It is not possible for anyone to meet our unresolved infant needs. The only one who can do that is Jesus Christ.

If a mother did not receive what she needed in the first months of her own life, she will have difficulty meeting the needs of her baby. Parents tend to wound their children at the very age they were wounded. It is very difficult for parents to give what has not been deposited in their lives: they give what has been given to them (see Gen. 8:22; Gal. 6:7—the law of sowing and reaping). What has been sown into a life will provide like seed to be sown again into future lives.

Lifelong problems can result if babies are separated from their mothers during this time of life, especially if the mother is gone for several days. Babies at this stage do not perceive that they exist separately from their mother. If this part of a baby's self goes away for a long period of time, baby perceives a major part of himself or herself as not existing. If this separation is extended, it is possible for a baby to begin to deteriorate physically.[4] In adulthood, this problem manifests as an inability to understand his or her existence or define who he or she is apart from others.

Another major problem occurs in the lives of people whose mothers were unresponsive to their needs, either because mother consciously refused to provide them with nurturing, was oblivious to their needs, or was physically/emotionally incapacitated. Whether conscious or unconscious, the result was the same. The person was wounded, and for the rest of their lives they work to set up symbiotic relationships with others in order to try to meet their infant needs. You will be in bondage to the wounds of your infancy only to the extent that you do not allow the Lord to reveal Himself in these areas of woundedness and heal you and set you free.

Other problems result if you were either neglected and under-protected, or over-indulged and over-protected. Again, such a condition within the symbiosis results in a bondage that motivates you throughout life to set up symbiotic relationships with others where you end up being neglected and abandoned or overprotected and controlled (see Rom. 6:16; 2 Pet. 2:19).

The Word tells us that we are in bondage when we are enslaved to something or to somebody. We will see this later in Martha's story, which was introduced at the beginning of this chapter. Wounds inflicted on us in the symbiosis place us in bondage. We become enslaved. We are not free to develop and grow as God intended. We are unable to realize the fullness of what God has for our lives. Until we recognize this, accept it and stop denying our wounds, we are destined to remain slaves to these abuses and deficiencies.

A third category of symbiotic wounding occurs when an infant does not receive the proper parenting to become an independent person apart from mom—capable of thinking, problem solving and being responsible for his or her own behavior. This needs to occur with the resolution of symbiosis, which we will discuss in chapter 4: "Terrific Twos."

In the symbiotic relationship, the mother is the responsible one. If mothers are dependent on their children for *their* value and worth, they will have difficulty giving up the caretaker role as their children grow and mature. They may not know how to encourage this maturity and independence. Thus, their children remain in bondage to immaturity. They are never really free. They become oppressed by an unhealthy dependent relationship with mother. Even when they leave home as adults, they remain in bondage, controlled by the very thing God originally provided to ensure their survival. This bondage destroys the fullness of what God intended for their lives. Due to problems during development, most people set up symbiotic relationships with others at various points in life. Over the years of ministry, we have discovered that people choose friends, marriage partners, occupations and numerous other choices based on unresolved symbiotic needs.

KEITH'S STORY

After eight years of marriage, Keith had yet to feel truly emotionally connected to his wife. He reported never having had the deep emotional closeness to his wife that he had always desired and expected to have. He knew the Lord had a great deal more for them within their marriage relationship. Keith reported not feeling any aversion to women. In fact, he got along better with women than men. He had a close relationship with his mother, but he had no relationship with his father, who died when Keith was only three days old.

We prayed and asked the Lord to reveal the root of his problem. Immediately, the Lord brought to Keith's memory the fact that he lost his father to a tragic accident only three days after his birth. As we asked the Lord to reveal what He wanted to show Keith about this time, he began to feel his mother's grief at the loss of her husband. He felt her fear, as well. Then, as he was experiencing all the emotions from his mom, he became aware of an intense desire to take care of his mother. At that moment, three-day-old Keith became his mom's caretaker. He took on the role of comforting her, protecting her and basically being to her what his father could no longer be. This role of being an emotional comforter and caretaker remained deeply entrenched and was not set aside when Keith got married. Therefore, he was not free to connect emotionally to his wife because his mother already occupied that place.

The Lord revealed Himself to three-day-old Keith and showed that, in fact, He was Keith's mother's comforter, protector and caretaker. Keith released his mom to Jesus and felt assured that the Lord would be her husband (see Isa. 54:5). Keith felt release as the drive to care for his mother was removed by the Lord's presence and assurance. Finally, he prayed to break off all ungodly symbiotic bondages between him and his mother, and to be fully connected to his wife in the deep emotional areas once occupied by his mother.

Today, Keith reports that a major change has occurred in his feelings of closeness to his wife. He is more involved, interactive and responsive to her needs. His wife previously reported that she saw no problem in their relationship. This was because she knew him in no other way. Yet, after the Lord set Keith free and healed him, she says he is much more involved at an emotional level. "I really enjoy my new husband!" she said.

JOSEPH'S STORY

Joseph suffered from fourth-stage colon cancer and was given only a few months to live. His pastor, church community and family prayed fervently in faith for his healing. Joseph had an impression that the Lord would heal him in the Healing Seminar. At the end of the seminar, he still had not been healed. So we met with Joseph and his wife and began to pray, asking the Holy Spirit to reveal the root of this cancer. The Lord showed us a blockage in Joseph that was preventing his healing. We continued to pray and ask the Holy Spirit to show us what happened to cause this.

Joseph saw himself as an infant, lying still and silent in a crib. Joseph's father had left them before he was born. His mother fell into deep depression and grief after Joseph was born, and was unable to care for him. Sensing his mother's pain, Joseph began to hold back his bowels and never cry, to make it easier for her. That heart impression in infancy created a toxic block in his body. The root of Joseph's cancer was from his unhealthy symbiosis with his mother. Through the symbiotic bond, Joseph received the impression that he needed to take care of her to survive. So he did all he could to help her.

Joseph asked Jesus to be there and show him what the Father wanted for him then. Jesus came to Joseph, took him in His arms and held him close. He told Joseph it was not his fault that his father left. It was not his responsibility to take care of his mother. Jesus told him, "I will take care of your mother; I want you to receive the care you need." In the arms of Jesus, Joseph visibly relaxed and received the care he had longed for his whole life. In that place of safety, Joseph took authority in Jesus' name and broke the heart vow he made to hold back his bowels and not cry. He gave his mother and all her needs to Jesus and broke the unhealthy symbiosis with her. He asked the Lord to uproot every lie in his heart from that experience and plant the truth. Then Joseph asked Jesus to heal him. In that moment, he felt a sensation like water flowing through his body.

He needed to stay in the manifest presence of the Lord. So Joseph went home to lie down on his bed. The sensation continued through the night. The next morning, he was scheduled for an MRI to check on the advancement of the cancer and discuss medications to minimize pain. Medically, there was no hope. His wife called when they returned home . . . ecstatic, hardly able to speak . . . they did the MRI, *twice*. The medical team could not believe it. The cancer was gone. The doctors were shocked. Joseph had a perfect colon. Jesus healed him, just as He promised.

A few years later, we received word from them; he was well and transformed. Before, Joseph hardly ever talked. He was always quiet and listening but did not say much. Since his healing, his wife says he talks all the time. She has to adjust to her new husband. Both blocks were removed and Joseph was truly free and living out his new freedom.

Sometimes the root of a physical problem is in the soul or spirit. In Joseph's case, the root of his problem was the wound from the unhealthy symbiosis. Once the root was revealed, and the Lord healed him and set him free, the physical problem was healed. Getting to the *real* root of the problem releases the breakthrough.

We can all receive the healing we need for the wounds we suffered during symbiosis. We can all be free of the bondages that imprison us in a continuous pattern of immaturity, failure, pain and suffering, and that prevent us from experiencing the fullness of life's joy and the fulfillment of God's purposes for us.

Wounds from the Feeding Process
We have already established that infants who did not make the connection between hunger pangs, crying and sucking experience problems in their adult lives with thinking, problem solving and effectively dealing with the issues of life. The most prevalent and

major wound is inflicted by the use of scheduled feeding methods. This type of regime causes people to learn that solving problems is beyond their control and relegated to the control of others. It promotes pessimism, passivity and a fatalistic attitude to life's problems.

God has built a unique "feeding schedule" into each child's life to sustain his or her individual development, growth and maturity. Mom needs to learn this schedule. Babies should not be controlled by an imposed time frame designed for mom's convenience, which ignores a baby's unique developmental needs. For example, if babies are placed on a four-hour feeding schedule but are hungry in three hours, they experience a great deal of pain and thus cry for an hour before they are fed. In this setup, they learn that their needs and feelings are not important and they internalize the belief that they do not matter to anyone. They also learn that it takes too much energy to solve problems.

If this happened to you, you may have grown up feeling controlled by others. As a result, you will tend to be passive, ignore your feelings and avoid dealing with problems. You avoid problems because you feel there is just no possible way to do anything effective to solve them. Scheduled feeding cripples people later in life in the areas of appropriate feeling, thinking and doing, causing them difficulty in being effective and responsible.

Feeding can also cause another type of problem in a child's development. If babies are on a three-hour feeding schedule but do not become hungry for four hours, they never really experience the pain of hunger. They are not provided with the opportunity to make the connection between hunger, crying and sucking to solve problems. When they become adults, such people may find themselves unable to identify feelings and, thus, are unable to discern accurately how to respond to life's issues and problems. They may ignore problems to such an extent that they get hurt, and so do their loved ones. They lack a fundamental skill for adult thinking and problem solving, which can be extremely tormenting as well as dangerous.

Every infant is entitled to the freedom to discover his or her own feelings, thinking and doing without being oppressed by the external controls of a caretaker. The best feeding method is demand feeding, which allows babies to get in touch with their internal needs and learn to be effective in getting their needs met. This provides an excellent foundation for effective thinking and problem solving.

Damage as a Result of Control
Too much control at this age sets a foundation for all future stages of development, causing young children to begin to relinquish control of their internal impulses and processes to mother and thereafter to all authority figures. We have witnessed the implications of this in our ministry. Having learned to give up internal impulse control to an external source at this young age, these individuals will always require someone else to monitor and correct their behavior and will have difficulty developing self-discipline. This is because their mother failed to allow them to develop their own control.

What we sow, we reap (see Gal. 6:7). If your mother imposed controls on you at a time when you needed to establish your own built-in ways of dealing with the world, you will have learned how to be self-indulgent and controlling of others. This will cause you difficulty in learning the basic foundational Christian principles of fully giving your life to Jesus, crucifying self and giving to others. But if parents and authority figures respected your needs at this crucial time of your life, you will have grown up learning to respect authority and to be aware of the needs of others. We believe such fruit is what all parents want for their children.

AGNES'S STORY (CONTINUED)

Agnes asked the Lord to reveal where her problem first took root in her life. The Lord revealed to her a time when she was about four or five months old. Agnes reported, "I'm just lying there crying. I'm not hungry. I need some attention, to be picked up and held. I'm crying. There's a man standing over me. He seems afraid to pick me up." At that moment the Lord revealed to Agnes that the man standing over her was her father. Agnes continued, "All of a sudden, my father leaves. He just walks away, leaving me crying. I feel fear and hatred of men taking root."

Crying Requires Response

There is a general belief that there is no harm in allowing babies to cry for long periods of time in the first six months of life, perhaps allowing them to cry themselves to sleep. Some people also believe that babies control their parents by crying. As we see in Agnes's case, infants have a different "belief." It is important to keep two considerations in mind: first, crying is the way babies communicate; second, how those caring for them respond to their crying affirms or undermines their existence. Thus, when babies are appropriately responded to, they are affirmed in their existence and encouraged to communicate their feelings.

When Crying Turns to Rage

We have ministered to many adults who have struggled with rage all their lives. Rage is a much more intense feeling than anger. It is uncontrollable and explodes from a person. One minute the person appears calm, the next minute he or she is overcome by violent emotion, often in response to frustrations or conflicts in life. Where the appropriate response might be anger or frustration, these people explode with rage.

Rage can be external or internal. Internal rage implodes within a person and creates severe pressure in the body, often resulting in stress disorders over time—high blood pressure, digestion problems, cardiovascular disorders, headaches, ulcers, and so on. The person who rages internally holds it inside, often because it was not safe to express it outwardly, or expressed negative emotions were not acceptable in the family or culture. As we've prayed with people who suffer from this problem and explore the leading of the Holy Spirit, we are always directed to focus back on the early months of the person's life. Rage is a feeling that is incorporated by the infant within the first three months of life. It happens like this.

When babies have a need, they cry to communicate the need. When no one responds, they will escalate the crying to signal the increased intensity of the feeling behind the need. When they are still not responded to, they begin to scream even more loudly to let someone know that if they are not cared for soon, they may not survive. The issue now becomes one of survival. It is a threat to their very existence. Hence, the fear of not surviving intensifies into desperation, and an all-out release of the urgency of the situation is now communicated.

When babies cry, they are communicating a need. They are not trying to control their parents. Crying is a God-given mechanism to signal their needs. At this age, the fulfillment of needs affirms the baby's existence and encourages him/her to survive. If no one responds, it threatens that very existence and survival. In order to find healing for the root of this problem, people need to return in their memory, in the Lord's presence, to the moment of time when the outbreak of rage occurred. The Lord Jesus reveals Himself to the crying infant and responds to his or her need. The Lord always reveals Himself to the screaming infant as the Father who cares and the one who will provide what he or she needs in this moment of time.

Rage causes significant harm to a person, emotionally, relationally and/or physically. So it is also wise to ask Jesus to heal and restore all that has been damaged.

When Crying Turns to Passivity

There is another problem that comes from your cries not being responded to in infancy. Your temperament may be more sensitive, and for you the response is not rage but rather passivity. *No one hears me, no one cares, so I'll just give up and become passive.* A type of helplessness settles in your heart and a powerlessness to communicate needs. Later in life, the pattern of passivity hinders your communication. Problems trigger the passive response. You need to be set free from the lie that no one cares and no one understands you, that you can't communicate. Jesus cares, He understands you, and you can communicate your needs to Him.

Let's return to infant Agnes, whose father ignored her crying.

AGNES'S STORY (CONTINUED)

Agnes again saw the picture of herself in her crib, crying to be held. When she asked the Lord to reveal Himself, she experienced Him pick her up, wrap His arms around her and hold her close. He spoke gently to her in comforting tones. His peace quieted her anxious heart. She could finally let go and relax: she was cared for.

Months later, Agnes sent us a testimony:

Gone is the fear and hatred of men. Gone is the desire to look for helpless, useless men to take care of. The Lord has shown me how to communicate with men; how to affirm men and communicate with them; how to communicate my needs without fear; how to affirm and encourage men to be what God wants them to be. Now, when I see a needy man, I pray for him. I see men in a totally different way now. I am capable of relationship with men without feeling fear, hatred or a motivation to care for them because of their helplessness. Most exciting is my relationship to Father God. I never realized how distant I was from the Father until after my healing time of prayer. Now I feel much closer to Him than ever before. I am really feeling truly connected to Him now.

This is what it's all about. Allow the Lord to take care of the wounds in life that have pulled you further and further away from Him.

Father God's Intervention

Unless the Lord intervenes, bringing new life and His healing touch into these areas of woundedness, these same wounds will be repeated in future generations. The major premise of this book is that all of us have been wounded in childhood. Yet, if we allow Him to, the Lord will heal us and set us free from the bondages of these wounds that hold us back from becoming all He intended us to be.

MARTHA'S STORY (CONTINUED)

During ministry, Martha began to recognize that immediately at birth she felt strong expectations for performance. She knew her parents wanted a girl and got her. At birth, and within the symbiosis, she experienced major pressure to live up to her mother's expectations of what she believed her daughter should be like. From the beginning Martha felt a strong demand to be the perfect baby girl. Then, the Lord revealed something to Martha. She saw that there was an oppressive heaviness around her neck and shoulders, crushing the life out of her. A yoke of slavery had been placed around her neck. This yoke was all the expectations to be the perfect daughter, which had been heaped onto her by her mother. But that wasn't all. This yoke of slavery was perpetuated by fear, anxiety and a deep sense of shame at even the thought of failure.

As we continued to pray, Martha shared what she was experiencing:

I actually experienced Father God announcing my birth with great joy to everyone around. The Lord took me from my mother's womb and held me in His arms, close to His chest. There is such a look of love and overwhelming pride on His face for me, His daughter Martha. The only possible posture I can take at this moment is to just be . . . I don't have to perform for His love; I'm just born, and I can't. Yet, He is bursting with joy in the simple fact that I am brought forth into this world. What love I feel!! What freedom!! I didn't do a single solitary thing to deserve this love. The yoke of slavery I've carried around my neck for 34 years is shattered! It has fallen away! Along with the yoke went the fear, anxiety and the shame of failure.

Five years later, Martha reports her testimony to God's faithfulness:

> In one word, FREEDOM! Freedom to try, freedom to fail, freedom to receive love from others without questioning it. Freedom to like myself. Freedom to say no without fearing rejection. The pivotal point is the major change I have experienced in my thought life. God likes me! Just the way I am. He really likes me! This thought has lifted the perpetual darkness that crept into my life whenever I fell short of perfection. There is Light now! I want to live life and somehow give out hope to others.

Even as this book is being written, Martha and her family are ministering to the destitute people in Bosnia-Herzegovina. She is living the opportunity she desired with all her heart—to share with others what was deposited into her life by Father God and to minister hope to the hopeless. Thanks be to our wonderful Lord!

Martha is just one of many people the Lord has touched and set free. Agnes and Keith can also be added to this list. We have consistently witnessed the Lord take broken, wounded lives and restore them to vibrant health. How faithful the Lord is to reveal Himself in every painful situation of our wounded past! He touches these times of pain and brings restoration and new life. There is nothing the Lord cannot touch and heal. And He never refuses to heal the wounds that cause the pain and the many tears of our young lives. In fact, He assures us of just the opposite:

> Record my lament; list my tears on your scroll—are they not in your record? (Ps. 56:8).

> Then those who feared the Lord talked with each other, and the Lord listened and heard. A scroll of remembrance was written in his presence concerning those who feared the Lord and honored his name (Mal. 3:16).

> This is what the Lord, the God of your father David, says: I
> have heard your prayer and seen your tears; I will heal you
> (2 Kings 20:5).

There is nothing that can prevent you from receiving your healing from the Lord.

Truth: Facing the Pain
Consider the adult problems identified in this chapter. Do you rec-
ognize any of these feelings, thoughts and behaviors in your life?
Review the Tables: Healthy/Unhealthy Development and ask the
Lord to show you if any of these apply to your life. Truth is the only
way to freedom.

Revelation: Revisiting the Scene
What happened in our infancy is a mystery to us. Cognitive recall is
not developed in the early months of life, yet the experiences of this
time leave an indelible impression in our being that affects us even
into adult life. We need the Holy Spirit to reveal what took root in
our lives in these early months. The Lord promises in His Word:

> He reveals deep and hidden things; he knows what lies in
> darkness, and light dwells with him (Dan. 2:22).

> For there is nothing hidden that will not be disclosed, and
> nothing concealed that will not be known or brought out
> into the open (Luke 8:17).

> Ask and it will be given to you (Matt. 7:7).

Redemption: Healing and Deliverance
Redemption rescues us from the loss of trust, the loss of the ability
to solve problems effectively, the loss of self-esteem, and the loss of
the ability to communicate with confidence. The Father longs to
heal us and provide the care we needed but didn't receive in the symbiosis. Our ability to trust—even to trust God—is affected by what

happened to us during this time. So it is easy to see why this stage is so important to us and to our relationship to the Father. Our eternal Father always hears us when we cry, and He answers us.

> O people of Zion, who live in Jerusalem, you will weep no more. How gracious he will be when you cry for help! As soon as he hears, he will answer you (Isa. 30:19).

Restoration: The Planting of the Lord
The process of restoration begins to take effect as Jesus reveals the Father to us. As we relive this phase of life with Jesus, He supernaturally imparts into our lives what the Father always wanted us to have. The old hurtful images and lies of the past give way to the new, life-giving experience in the presence of the Lord, making us whole again.

Reparenting: Father God, "Father" Us
Healing and deliverance free us to begin to grow up. Restoration begins when the Lord uproots the weeds of destruction and plants the seeds of newness of life. Another hindrance to maturity is removed when we realize that we have the power to walk free. Our relationship with the Father is vital after receiving healing of the wounds that occurred at this time of our development. Draw near to Him and come to know Him as He really is. Trust and faith develop through intimacy. As the Father fathers us, our infant needs are satisfied, our anxious hearts are quieted and the peace that passes understanding secures our life in Him.

THE FATHER'S HEALING PROCESS:
STEPS TO HEALING, FREEDOM AND RESTORATION

Healing
1. Identify the adult problems—feelings, thoughts, behaviors that apply to you from this stage of development. (See Tables 2A/2B: Healthy/Unhealthy Development.)

2. Ask the Holy Spirit to reveal the root cause of each problem. The root is whatever happened to you from birth to six months that caused a wounding in your life and allowed the problem to take root. This revelation may be in the form of a memory, a picture, an impression, a thought, an awareness, or some other way of "knowing" (see Luke 8:17).

3. Ask Jesus to reveal His Presence there with you. The Lord never changes, but His presence changes things (see Ps. 31:14-16; Heb. 13:5-6,8).

4. Tell Jesus what you are feeling and thinking in this revealed time, place, experience. Listen to His response (see Pss. 88:1; 91:14-16).

5. Ask Jesus to reveal what the Father intended for this time of your life. Jesus comes to show us the Father. Allow the Lord to minister to you; rest in Him and take time to receive what you needed in early life. Let it go deep into your heart. He comes to care for your developmental needs, to heal you, to redeem all that was lost to you and to restore you to be all He created you to be (see Jer. 29:11; Matt. 15:13).

Freedom

6. In the name of Jesus, break the power of the lie that was planted in your heart from the wound and ask the Lord to uproot it. Embrace the truth—the Word of God—that has the power to set you free. Proclaim the promises in God's Word that are His answers to your need (see Matt. 15:13; John 8:31-32; 2 Cor. 1:20).

7. Identify any patterns of sin, bondage or curses passed from generation to generation in your family. Break any generational curses, if necessary (see also Appendix A: Generational Curses). Forgive your parents and all those who wounded you (see Matt. 6:14; Gal. 3:13-14).

8. Take authority, in Jesus' name, over any demonic oppression or influences in your life that the Lord has revealed. In the name of Jesus and His authority, command them to leave (see Luke 10:19; Jas. 4:7).

Restoration

9. Receive Father God as your eternal Father and receive your inheritance of life in Christ Jesus. Seek the Father each day and ask Him to father you (see John 10:10; Heb. 12:10).

10. Ask the Holy Spirit to teach you how to walk in your "newness of life." Commit to listen to and obey the Holy Spirit and begin to put God's Word into action in your life (see John 14:26; 16:13; Phil. 2:12-13).

Table 2A: Healthy Development

Stage of Life	Significant Issues	Developmental Task (needed for healthy development)	Adult Manifestation
Birth to 6 Months	Existence/ basic trust Self-concept foundation Problem-solving foundation Foundation for communication	Healthy symbiosis with mother Receive unconditional love Define internal and external existence Integrate feeling, thinking, doing Incorporate communication skills	Trust others Establish healthy relationships Secure in relationships Identify feelings Communicate needs and feelings Aware of internal and external boundaries Trust God

Table 2B: Unhealthy Development

Stage of Life	Significant Issues	Developmental Task (needed for healthy development)	Adult Manifestation
Birth to 6 Months	Existence/ basic trust Self-concept formation Problem-solving foundation Foundation for communication	Disturbances in symbiosis with mother Parent-imposed feeding schedules Parent-imposed expectations Inappropriate response to cry Reaction that increases discomfort Unresponsiveness Internal disturbance and pain	Lack ability to trust Father God Rage Discount problems Difficulties in relationships Lack ability to trust Problems with thinking and problem solving Discount feelings Poor self-concept Unable to communicate needs

EXPLORATION

Six to Eighteen Months

"NO!" The shock of his mother's shout jolted Peter back from yet another futile attempt at exploring the world around him. He was confused, frustrated and itching to relieve the energy inside. Fifteen-month-old Peter experienced many such encounters with his parents. They were professionals who were very successful and very much in control of their lives. They were highly respected by all who knew them. Yet, without realizing it, the pervasive pressure of their control was slowly and systematically crushing Peter's curiosity and desire to explore, and tragically undermining the healthy development of his motivation, initiative, mobility and creativity.

The exploratory stage of development from 6 to 18 months is a dynamic period of life, rich with wonder and an intrinsic desire to experience and explore the world. Exploration's primary goals are to develop self-initiative, self-motivation, concept learning and mobility. The most important requirements for healthy development now are permission and protection in exploration. Self-initiative and self-motivation need to be encouraged without performance expectations, punishment or excessive restriction. At this stage, loss of parental nurturing, long periods of confinement and oppressive control, as well as performance expectations, punishment and lack of protection in exploration often result in wounding that affects behavior later in life.

Adult Problems

As an adult, Peter came to us for ministry and counsel. His jaw flexed as he shared the struggle he was having dealing with the authority figures in his life. Frustration and anger were feelings that were all too familiar to him.

Throughout his life people in authority were either controlling him or criticizing him for not having any initiative or motivation. He felt driven to please others. Self-awareness and the Lord's direction for his life were muddled by the onslaught of the expectations and demands of others. It was true: Peter needed to get in touch with his initiative and self-motivation. Not only was he controlled by others, but he also allowed it. It was frustrating and oppressive to him; yet, paradoxically, it was what he found to be most familiar to him. He was either being told what to do and when to do it or being criticized and reprimanded for not taking initiative. Finally, living in this "double bind" had taken its toll— the stress was unbearable.

Peter was an oppressed, demotivated people-pleaser in bondage to the expectations and control of others. There are many such Peters in this world with similar stories. We will return to Peter's story later in the chapter.

What happened in your development during this time of exploration? The results are manifested in your life today. Do you lack initiative and motivation? Do you find it difficult to hear the voice of God and sense His direction in your life? Do you find it difficult to know what you are feeling? Is your behavior motivated by the fear of rejection or abandonment? Have you learned how to please others to the exclusion of your own needs for a balanced, healthy life? Do you see a pattern in your life where people take advantage of you? Do you frequently feel overwhelmed or smothered by circumstances or the people closest to you? Do you struggle with passivity, over adaptation, anxiety or immobilization? The answers to many of these questions concerning the roots of such adult life manifestations can be found in understanding your developmental process between the period of time when you were 6 to 18 months of age.

Developmental Process

The exploration stage of development is a time when the world suddenly comes into vibrant focus and we are drawn out from our self-absorption to explore the wonders all around us. It is a time to experience and develop initiative, motivation, mobility, creativity and an understanding of spatial and conceptual relationships. The problems and frustrations we encounter as we explore the world all help in the process of learning what we can and cannot do.

At this stage of development, we are working through symbiosis and beginning to do things on our own. In order to succeed, we need to be encouraged. It is essential that we learn that exploring and developing will not result in abandonment, punishment or loss of nurturing. Unconditional love is required at this stage to maximize a child's healthy development.

Before you read further, think about this past year. How many people with whom you came in frequent contact were highly motivated, full of initiative and very creative? What percentage of people would you say have these attributes? Maybe 3 to 5 percent? Or maybe up to 10 percent? Why are so few people highly motivated, full of initiative and creative? Let's look at the reasons.

The Exploration Stage

We will only become self-motivated and creative adults who are able to take initiative if we are allowed to explore the "world" at this important phase of our lives. These characteristics must be established, encouraged and rewarded. Getting in touch with our motivation and initiative helps us get in touch with ourselves.

We have consistently found that self-motivation, self-initiative and creativity get snuffed out of people's lives. Why? Due to a lack of understanding, parents, in their zeal to discipline, inadvertently destroy motivation, initiative and creativity. Inappropriate parenting can have a devastating effect on budding individuality.

It is important to be allowed and even encouraged to use our own natural motivation rather than have to respond to the expectations and motivations of others. It is at this exploration stage that these vital attributes begin and are encouraged to flourish or are discouraged and wither away. Getting in touch with our inner motivation and initiative helps us get in touch with ourselves. Through exploration, we discover what we can and cannot do.

Conceptualizing the World

Personal experience is the best way to discover the world. While primary needs for nurture remain important, we begin to conceptualize the world around us through exploration. We learn the meaning of important concepts like near/far, over/under, hard/soft, hot/cold, big/little, crash/splash. We want to know what is under, behind, on top of, inside of every object we encounter. Curiosity about everything prompts mobility. We become "little explorers."

During these months of life we are best described as a "touching machine." We live to touch, and we touch to live. This burst of energy and activity creates new challenges for parents. By giving us permission to explore, they are stimulating our learning; by providing us with protection, they are preventing the occurrence of wounding experiences that might cause us to shut down inside.

Science Confirms the Importance of Exploration

Scientific research in recent years has underscored how critically important this phase of child development is. At this stage the nervous system and muscle coordination are developing at their most rapid rate, with neural connections being formed at an explosive rate. Research reported in *Time* magazine states:

> "What wires a child's brain," say neuroscientists, "is repeated experience. Each time a baby tries to touch a tantalizing object, or gazes intently at a face or listens to a lullaby, tiny bursts of electricity shoot through the brain, knitting neurons into circuits as well defined as those etched in silicon chips."[1]

If these connections are to become permanently established, they must be exercised by stimulation. The more the child is allowed to explore, touch and manipulate objects, the more neural connections are formed and the more enriched the nervous system becomes. The research of William Greenough, of the University of Illinois, confirms this: "A lot of organization (in the brain) takes place using information gleaned from when the child moves about in the world. If you restrict activity, you inhibit the formation of synaptic connections in the cerebellum."[2] If neural connections are not stimulated and exercised through exploration, touch and manipulation, they deteriorate, atrophy or waste away, and the nervous system becomes starved. The resulting deprivation is significant enough to cause problems later in life with reading, writing, thinking, conceptualizing and nearly all forms of learning.[3] Deprived of a stimulating environment, the child's brain suffers. Researchers at Baylor College of Medicine, for example, have found that the brains of children who don't play much or are rarely touched are 20 percent to 30 percent smaller than normal for their age.[4] In contrast, babies who are given permission to explore within the freedom of a protected environment thrive.

Foundations for Adult Problem-Solving

This is a critical time for the formation of spatial and conceptual relationships, which are foundational in the development of all future thinking, learning and problem solving.[5]

In learning to understand spatial relationship, we become aware of how objects are set up in space. How is a chair positioned in relationship to the floor and the table? How is the sofa positioned in relationship to the wall? How much space is there between the wooden bars on the railing of the stairs? In order to assess these relationships, we must crawl or walk over to the object and explore its relationship to other things. So we push and squeeze our little bodies between the couch and the wall or stick our heads between the stair railing bars and get stuck. In this way we gain a personal understanding of spatial relationships.

These early discoveries are vital if we are to think and solve problems effectively later in life. If we are restricted in how much we are allowed to explore by controlling, dominating or overprotective parents, our spatial relationship skills do not develop sufficiently, which may result in difficulties with learning and problem solving later in life.

Developing the Ability to Imagine

Conceptual relationships are also being developed at this stage. This is the ability to think about objects or places when they are no longer in our immediate surroundings. It is the ability to imagine. If we try to think about a place without having been there, we are unable to create an accurate image in our minds. If we have not explored something, seen it or had the opportunity to experience it, we will be unable to conceptualize it. Conceptualization, essentially, is the ability to create an image of something in our mind, and it is an important tool in thinking effectively and functioning adequately in life.

Restricted mobility during this stage, or the unavailability of objects to manipulate and explore, can seriously affect our ability to function in this area. Being confined for long periods of time to "baby jail," commonly known as a playpen, or in "bungee bondage," hanging from a suspended rubber-banded swing in a doorframe, seriously restricts mobility and hinders exploration, causing conceptual and spatial relationship deficiencies.

Exploring the Existence of Things

Up to this stage, "out of sight" was "out of mind"—the person or the object no longer existed when out of view. Now we learn that people can leave a room and still exist, and that things can be put away and still exist. Play involves putting things in places and taking them out again. We are working at developing fantasies and images regarding objects and the constancy of objects. This is the time when people play peek-a-boo with us and enjoy watching us laugh and we get excited when they suddenly reappear.[6]

JACK'S STORY

We ministered to a young man, Jack, who had feared abandonment all his life. The Lord revealed to him—and later it was confirmed by his parents—that prior to seven months old, and for a period of several months, he was frequently left with his grandparents on weekends while his parents went away. When the parents returned to retrieve Jack from his grandparents, they would find him reluctant to come to them. Jack appeared not to recognize his mom and dad. This occurred because Jack had not yet developed the cognition for "constancy of objects." His parents were, in a sense, unfamiliar to him because he did not remember them. Basically, Jack experienced abandonment, as all children of this age will if left by parents for extended periods of time.[7] In healing prayer, Jack experienced the presence of the Lord with him, caring for him when his parents left, healing the break in the bonding, releasing him from the fear of abandonment.

Messy but Necessary

We need freedom to be who God made us to be. We need to develop in the ways God has set within every human being. Now is the time for mess. It is important to be able to be messy without feeling parental rejection or repulsion. This stage may also be referred to as the "baptismal" stage of development.

At this age, we enjoy spilling everything. It is exciting to watch all the wonderful things that milk, juice, soup, and so on, do when they splash. Smashing and squashing food produces exciting new discoveries. If given the opportunity, we make a great deal of mess. The dried-on food decorating our face and hair adds to the messy look. This is developmentally normal, occurring around eight to ten months and continuing for several months. Unconditional love and attention are needed now more than ever.

How mom reacts to us makes an indelible impression on our thoughts, feelings and behavior, since the symbiosis between the mother and child is at its strongest.[8] If she reacts positively, our self-image is enhanced; but if she reacts negatively, it is diminished.

Testing Separation

At 15 to 20 months, exploration really picks up. We are working through the symbiosis when we depended on mom for everything, to find out about separation. We are discovering what we can and cannot do. More than ever, we need to experience encouragement, freedom and support as we explore.[9] This is not the time for increased punishment, discipline or undue restriction in mobility. What is important now is appropriate protection in exploration, but avoiding the extremes of overprotection (that is, smothering and restriction) or a lack of protection (neglect and unresponsiveness). Either extreme adversely affects the quality of our exploration and ultimately undermines the development of maximum brain function.

Mom, I Want to Feed Myself!

Some time around 10 to 12 months old, we need to be allowed and encouraged to feed ourselves. Feeding is another significant activity that encourages self-motivation and self-initiative through exploration.

Some children may be prevented from doing this because it's too messy or because they don't get enough food in their mouths. Rather than discouraging the child's desire, it is more appropriate for child and parent each to have a spoon—which will ensure that at least some of the food will be eaten.

Let's consider now what can go wrong at this age and what impact this may have on healthy adult functioning.

Weeds and Roots

PETER'S STORY

When Peter was a child, he was very active and curious. He would get into anything he could. The Lord revealed to him the extreme intensity with which his mother and father would stop him from exploring. He once again experienced the long-forgotten shock of his mother's piercing scream riveting him to the spot, cutting short his attempts at exploration.

What Happened to My Motivation?

If mobility is restricted, and if permission to explore is replaced with constant discipline and punishment, we won't discover our capabilities and grow in self-motivation. Self-initiative and spatial and conceptual relationships will also suffer. If every effort to explore our world is stopped by "NO!" without any "YES" to redirect our energy, the energy diffuses in us and can cause us to be agitated, hyperactive and unable to focus.

As a result of my experience as a school psychologist for 15 years, I found that some learning disabilities are functional—related to inappropriate parenting—rather than organic in nature. As a result of inappropriate, ineffective parenting at this stage, children develop difficulties with focus, attention and learning later in life.

"Stop This Mess!"

There is a danger that during this "messy" stage, you may have received the impression from mom that something was wrong with you, that you were not right for her somehow. You may have received these messages if you had a "super clean" mom who always cleaned you up immediately whenever there was the slightest mess. Such behavior instills a sense of rejection of who and what you are. The nagging perception and belief that you are *not right*, that something is wrong with you, was impressed upon your developing awareness and image of yourself. You were not accepted for who you were or who you were becoming.

Does this sound familiar to you now as an adult?

LINDA'S STORY

Linda experienced rejection from her mother at this "messy" time of her life. She grew up with the obsessive belief that no one accepted who she was, especially authority figures. She had the self-perception that she was somehow dirty or unclean. She believed that no one could ever really love or appreciate her for *who* she was. She had received strong messages that she could not be who God had naturally made her to be, and she felt that she needed to be something other than who she was to gain love and acceptance. God calls this "man pleasing."[10] Psychologists call this abandoning one's own identity.

When Linda asked the Holy Spirit to reveal the root cause of this, she saw a picture of herself as a baby. Every time Linda was the least bit messy, her mom looked at her in disgust, mumbled something and wiped her face or body until she felt it burn from the rubbing. She asked the Lord to reveal Himself in that time and show her what the Father wanted for her then. The Lord stepped in between Linda and her mom. He took the cloth from her mom and told her He would take care of Linda.

Linda re-experienced this time with the Lord. Although she was messy, He smiled at her and looked at her with great love. He even encouraged her to be messy. He loved and delighted in her in the midst of her messiness. Linda felt the knot in her stomach relax. She was set free by the Lord. His acceptance of her even in her messiness was just what she needed to break free from the bondage of rejection. She was free to accept herself for who the Lord made her to be. No longer expecting rejection, she could begin to learn how to receive acceptance from herself and others.

Parents don't always consider the long-term effect on their children of what they say and do. They are then surprised when the fruit of what they have planted in their children's lives begins to manifest itself in later life. Children base their impressions, feelings and beliefs about themselves on their perceptions of how they are treated by those caring for them and what is said to them.

"Don't Touch!"

Consider this real-life situation. I am 15 months old, and you are my parent. You take me into a crystal and china store. You have now created a problem for yourself and me if you expect me not to touch anything. Remember, I am a "touching machine." You now tempt my natural desire to touch and explore. I will go after everything in the store. To prevent me from breaking something, what must you do? You will need to continually tell me "NO!" to stop me from touching. This will frustrate my innate desire to explore. If you do not want me to touch, either hold me while we are in the store or, better still, don't take me in the store at all. But please, don't put me down on the floor and expect me not to touch. This is unrealistic and will only result in frustration for both of us.

God does not tempt us, and neither should an adult tempt a 15-month-old child to stop doing what he or she is meant to do at this stage of life.

Exactly What Part of "No" Don't You Understand?

Consider another real-life situation. Again, I am fifteen months old, and I go to touch something. You tell me "NO!" I go to touch something else, and again you tell me "NO!" If there are numerous "blocks" like this throughout my day, what will happen to the energy in me that has not been given properly focused release? It remains inside me as undifferentiated and diffuse energy, which will manifest itself in my behavior as agitation. I will begin releasing it in unfocused, non-goal-directed ways. Does this sound familiar? It might be that my behavior and inability to focus my energy will lead to hyperactivity, which could then lead to a diagnosis of Attention Deficit Disorder, also known as ADD.

The Result of Too Much Control

Some parents misunderstand this stage and, as a result, they discipline, restrain and correct their child too often. They do this for a variety of reasons, but one of the main reasons is fear. Either parents fear that other people will think they are raising an undisciplined, uncontrolled child (fear of man), or they fear their child will get hurt (fear of harm), or that the child might destroy something (fear of loss). Fear, then, becomes the motivation behind parental correction. A child who is restrained by a parent from exploring, initiating and self-motivating out of fear will learn to connect these activities with fear. When carried into later life, fear is triggered in situations requiring these qualities, which will hold the individual back from functioning effectively and responsibly.

Does this strike a familiar chord with you? This is an issue we often encounter when ministering to people who have been subject to too much control during the exploratory stage of development.

Self-Feeding: Mom Has the Food

As we mentioned earlier, self-feeding is an activity that needs to be encouraged. If you were not allowed to explore self-feeding, you will have been discouraged from developing self-initiative and self-motivation, and encouraged to be dependent. This may have resulted in your incorporating the distorted perception into your thinking that dependency on parents or authority figures is an attribute that should be developed. This leads to the kind of situation where 35-year-old children are still living at home, expecting their parents to "feed them." Excessive control at this stage in a child's development can be devastating to budding initiative and motivation.

I Want to Do It Myself

If, when you were exploring the world and learning to perform such tasks as stacking blocks or putting pegs in holes, other people were constantly intruding and demonstrating the correct way to do it, you may have become demotivated. As a result, you may still have the feeling that you can't do things well, that you are not capable and that others can do things better than you. If there was too much intrusion in your activities, your autonomy, initiative and spontaneous motivation will probably have become diminished. Babies need autonomy to experience and manipulate objects within their environment.

Roots of Man-Pleasing

Some people were encouraged by their parents to act "cute." If your parents did this, you may have learned to perform for people and thus have become a man-pleaser (something God expressly forbids in Galatians 1:10). When you were required to act "cute" or perform for others, you were placed at risk. Your own initiative and spontaneous motivation were infringed upon; you learned to over-adapt to others; you learned to respond more to the demands of others than to your own internal processes.

As an adult, you function out of the motivation of others rather than out of your own motivation and self-initiative, which is undeveloped or underdeveloped (as we saw in Peter's story). Such people feel that their life is not their own—and it isn't. They have difficulty identifying their feelings and cannot seem to distinguish between their wants and their needs. They report having difficulty identifying what they need and asking for it. These people are always pulled along in life by the demands and expectations of others, rather than being prompted by motivation from within and the leading of the Holy Spirit. Without a developed internal awareness, it is difficult to hear the voice of God. When our focus is external, we are vulnerable to being controlled by others.

The Effect of Punishment at This Stage

During this exploration stage of a child's development it is very important that performance expectations are kept to a minimum. A heavy amount of discipline and punishment is also inappropriate. At 6 to 18 months, it is more appropriate for a child to be guided and redirected than to be heavily disciplined and punished for age-appropriate behavior. Structured, consistent discipline needs to begin when the child reaches the age of two. Punishment any earlier is a direct attack on the development of initiative, motivation, creativity and mobility.

If you were punished regularly at this age, you will have become demotivated, lacking in initiative and are either passive or hyperactive. You will also have become passive and prone to over-adapting to the demands and needs of others.

Parents appear to be the ones who benefit most from punishment at this stage. For the child, punishment only results in deactivating an otherwise active, curious human being.

Toilet Training Too Early

Between the ages of 6 and 18 months, children are not yet developmentally ready to begin toilet training.[11] All parent-initiated expectations should remain at a minimum to protect children from having to over-adapt to the wants and needs of others. The more we are required to over-adapt during this exploration stage, the more likely we are to develop a man-pleasing orientation to life, learning to discount our own needs and wants and operate out of others' needs and wants. This can cause a loss of sensitivity to our internal life and make it difficult to hear the voice of God as we mature.

The most destructive result of starting toilet training too early, however, is on the child's developing ability to learn self-control and impulse control. We have discovered that adults whose parents toilet trained them too early give up the self-initiative and motivation necessary to establish self-control. They essentially abandon self-control while over-adapting to the control of others.

If you struggle with such an orientation to life, you may struggle with an endless and frustrating cycle of sin and condemnation. Self-control/self-discipline—an important fruit of the Holy Spirit—will be totally missing from your life. However, do not despair; it is possible to develop this fruit of the Spirit in your life. Allow the Lord to reveal the wounds you suffered at this stage of life. He will uproot the destruction and redeem what was lost.

Father God's Intervention

PETER'S HEALING

During prayer and ministry, the Lord revealed Himself to Peter and stood between him and his mother. He experienced the Lord comforting his mother, reassuring her that Peter would not grow up to be undisciplined if she allowed him to explore now. He instructed her that Peter needed the freedom to explore and discover, without excessive correction and punishment, to be healthy and well developed. Then Jesus came to Peter and removed the invisible force of control and fear binding him. He was free. He felt the release and life stirring within him. The fire of initiative and motivation was burning again. He knew the Lord was encouraging him to move out, to be motivated once again to explore. Peter felt a huge, oppressive cloud lift from his life; he had never before experienced life without it. He felt energy return to his body. He felt fear flee as the Lord walked with him through several adventures in exploration. The Lord had reawakened Peter's initiative and motivation. He was free—free to experience the fullness of who he was created to be and what God originally intended for his life.

As we mature from a child to an adult, Father God wants each of us to be creative and motivated with a high degree of initiative.

Truth: Facing the Pain

Do others often explain the consequences of your behavior to you? If you are honest with yourself, do you expect others to modify your behavior rather than taking responsibility for it yourself? If you answered yes to either of these questions, it is a sure sign that your exploratory stage of development was unduly restricted and controlled. Developmentally inappropriate demands and expectations for performance were probably imposed on you. It is possible to be trained to behave in certain ways through "classical conditioning," even before cognitive cause-and-effect thinking has developed. We will discuss this in greater detail in the next chapter.

If you were classically conditioned at this stage in your development, you never really developed your own self-initiated skills to use in modifying your behavior. You gave up internal self-control of your behavior to adapt to external control. The external control now comes from authority figures who provide the primary source of motivation for the way you operate in life.

Revelation: Revisiting the Scene

Stop for a moment and ask the Holy Spirit to take you back to this time in your development and reveal anything that may have happened to wound you. Jesus wants to reveal the Father to you and parent you in the way He knew you needed for your healthy development. He will heal you, protect you from harm, set you free, uproot the destruction and supernaturally impart exactly what you needed for life and health at that time.

Redemption: Healing and Deliverance

The Father desires to set you free. He wants to heal your wounds. The Lord will minister to you back at the time when you were 6 to 18 months old. Father God knows what happened in your life to diminish who He made you to be. You may not be in touch with your inner self at all; you may even feel dead inside, without any sense of your own needs or feelings. It is essential to be connected to your internal life—to your heart—in order for you to hear the voice of God and be led by His Spirit. The Lord will uproot the destructive forces of control and fear and restore your desire to explore, with His protection. He will supernaturally impart what you needed to develop in your internal life as He originally intended.

Restoration: The Planting of the Lord

The Father wants to restore what was lost—your initiative, motivation and creativity. Most of all, He wants to breathe resurrection life into your inner self, your "heart life," so that you may hear His voice.

Reparenting: Father God, "Father" Us

The Father longs for you to develop in self-initiative, motivation and creativity and to be the person He created *you* to be. Freedom is only the beginning. He will be there to encourage and protect you in your renewed desire to develop your initiative, motivation and creativity. He will be there to speak to you in your heart and lead you by His Spirit.

THE FATHER'S HEALING PROCESS:
STEPS TO HEALING, FREEDOM AND RESTORATION

Healing

1. Identify the adult problems—attitudes and behaviors—that apply to you. (See Tables 3A/3B: Healthy/Unhealthy Development.)

2. Ask the Holy Spirit to reveal the root cause of each problem. The root is whatever happened to you between the ages of 6 to

18 months that caused a wounding in your life and allowed the problem to take root. This revelation may be in the form of a memory, a picture, an impression, a thought, an awareness or some other way of "knowing" (see Luke 8:17).

3. Ask Jesus to reveal His presence there with you. The presence of the Lord changes things (see Ps. 31:14-16; Heb. 13:5-6,8).

4. Tell Jesus what you are feeling and thinking in this revealed time, place, experience. Listen to His response (see Pss. 88:1; 91:14-16).

5. Ask Jesus to reveal what the Father intended for this time of your life. Jesus comes to show us the Father. Allow the Lord to minister to you; rest in Him and take time to receive what you need. He comes to care for your developmental needs, to heal you, to redeem all that was lost to you, and to restore you to be all He created you to be (see Jer. 29:11; Matt. 15:13).

Freedom

6. In the name of Jesus, break the power of the lie that was planted in your heart from the wound and ask the Lord to uproot it. Embrace the truth that has the power to set you free, the Word of God. Proclaim the promises in God's Word that are His answers to your need (see Matt. 15:13; John 8:31-32; 2 Cor. 1:20).

7. Identify any patterns of sin, bondages or curses that passed from generation to generation in your family. Break any generational curses, if necessary (see Appendix A: Generational Curses). Forgive your parents and all those who wounded you (see Matt. 6:14; Gal. 3:13-14).

8. Take authority, in Jesus' name, over any demonic oppression or influences in your life that the Lord has revealed. In the name and authority of Jesus, command them to leave (see Luke 10:19; Jas. 4:7).

Restoration

9. Receive Father God as your eternal Father, and receive your inheritance of life in Christ Jesus. Seek the Father each day to "father" you (see John 10:10; Heb. 12:10).

10. Ask the Holy Spirit to teach you how to walk in your "new-ness of life." Commit to listen to and obey the Holy Spirit, and begin to put God's Word into action in your life (see John 14:26; 16:13, Phil. 2:12-13).

Table 3A: Healthy Development

Stage of Life	Significant Issues	Developmental Task (needed for healthy development)	Adult Manifestation
6 Months to 18 Months	Exploration: mobility/ initiative/ motivation/ creativity Concept learning	Permission to explore Protection in exploration Explore self-motivation Learn spatial and conceptual relationships Explore self-initiative Unconditional positive affection	Active self-motivation, self-initiative Healthy social interaction Accept own wants and needs Balance in caring for self and others Sensitive to the Holy Spirit/ able to hear God's voice

Table 3B: Unhealthy Development

Stage of Life	Significant Issues	Developmental Task (needed for healthy development)	Adult Manifestation
6 Months to 18 Months	Exploration: mobility/ initiative/ motivation/ creativity Concept learning	Unhealthy symbiosis Learn dependency Lack of protection in exploration Restricted mobility Frequent punishment or discipline Performance expectations Premature toilet training	Lack motivation and initiative Lack impulse control Problems with control Lack self-control Feelings seen as problems and discounted until build up to eruption Relationships are symbiotic Man-pleasing/ over-adaptive Lack freedom in the Lord Difficulty hearing God's voice

BEGINNING INDEPENDENCE

Two Years of Age

MICHAEL'S STORY

"Michael! Come here right now!!" Michael stood firm . . . his toes gripped the carpet, rooted in opposition. Every command from his mother sparked all the two-year-old anger, resistance and defiance little Michael could muster. His mother, confronted with this challenge, perceived it as a threat to her supremacy in the home. Determined to maintain her iron grip, she escalated her anger to subdue him. These episodes only served to strengthen Michael in his resolve to fight the control. Michael had already learned to be very stubborn and rebellious because of all the control and mother domination he had lived with since birth. Again the battle was on. Mom vs. Michael, who would win?

Two years old. What a terrific, turbulent time of life! Time to break symbiosis with mom and become a separate person. Time to begin exercising our cognitive recall, also known as memory, and cause-and-effect thinking. Time to think and solve problems and become responsible for our own behavior. All these are important tasks now in development. It is time to get free of self-centeredness and establish a social contract—that is, to find out how to live in society and learn to cooperate and share with others. Struggles with control, with anger and with opposition displace the blissful days of exploration.

It's difficult to navigate these turbulent waters. Many get caught in the endless whirlpool of "self" and lose their way. It takes understanding and godly wisdom to hold the course steady and make it through this stage successfully. This time of life is extremely significant on our journey to maturity. Wounds inflicted at this age cause major stumbling blocks for many of us. How many of us have yet to resolve these issues as adults? Many are plagued with unresolved "two-year-old stuff" even in the later years of life. Some people never get victory in these areas, no matter how long they live.

Adult Problems

Acting in an inconsiderate way toward others; lacking self-discipline; being oppositional, negative, competitive, controlling and self-centered are the most obvious adult manifestations of wounds that were inflicted upon a child during this stage of life. Many adults still suffer from the two-year-old syndrome: "I want it my way!" They are angry, negative and oppositional, always confronting life's issues and problems with a pervasive drive to compete with and control others. These people frequently struggle to be free of what they perceive as oppressive demands on them. They control others to get what they want.

In the extreme, they are self-centered, abusive, narcissistic and demanding. They resist taking responsibility for their own feeling, thinking and doing and for the consequences of their behavior. They are involved in relationships where they can either control or be controlled by the other. In either relationship, they justify expressing their ever-present feelings of anger.

We believe that most of us have some of these issues going on in our lives. It is time to face the truth and deal with them. It is time to learn to take personal responsibility instead of blaming others. It's time to take action. Go after these issues in your life; allow the Lord to reveal the roots and heal the wounds. When people are set free of two-year-old stuff, the change is dramatic and life changing.

MICHAEL'S STORY (CONTINUED)

Michael was an angry, abusive, controlling husband. He came for ministry when his wife left him. He was shocked that she had abandoned him so abruptly. "After all these years, why did she just up and leave now?" Michael complained. He had been married for 20 years. He had no concept of the "we" aspect in the marriage relationship and no understanding of other people's feelings. All was done in his home the way he wanted it. He was not in the slightest bit aware just how self-centered and self-serving he was. No one ever confronted his selfishness because they feared his angry retaliation. Michael was not a very nice man. The worst part of it was, he did not even realize how obnoxious he was to others. In his blindness, he could not see that he had destroyed his marriage.

So, how can a person get "stuck" in two-year-old behavior?

Developmental Process

"NOOOO!" is the battle cry that resounds in the wake of little ones turned two as they dash away from mom. Overnight, it seems, they are transformed from sweet baby to tiny tyrant, becoming negative, oppositional and even rebellious. God has given the two-year-old a one-word gift. It is the same word He gives every two-year-old in every language all over the world. The word is "NO!"—and he or she uses it to reply to almost everything. Some people refer to this time as the "terrible twos," which is a decidedly negative perspective. We prefer to view this time as the "terrific twos."[1]

Much is happening inside the two-year-old. It is a dynamic stage of development. It is the birth of independence and the surging of individuality as our unique personality begins to take shape. Many changes are occurring in our world and in our body. There are social rules and behavioral demands to deal with. We are able to *begin* to discern right from wrong, and so we can begin to learn responsibility for our behavior. These new challenges, along with internal physiological changes, cause us a great deal of discomfort, resulting in anger.

The most dramatic opposition is with mom. As the need for the symbiosis required for survival earlier in life begins to break down, we begin to think independently and tackle small problems on our own. For example, we don't need mom to get all of our food—we know exactly where to go to get cookies! Parents, especially mom, can support their children by encouraging budding independence while continuing to love, care for and nurture—this is the parents' main task now. Toddlers need to learn that they can think independently and become separate, and yet still receive nurturing and care. Basically, the issue is, "Can I still get taken care of if I think for myself?"

Having lived their whole life within the symbiosis, challenging it is obviously a focus of concern, even fear. It is important for two-year-olds to learn that making decisions results in positive consequences.

Anger and the Social Contract

At 15 months old, we spill milk to watch it splash and learn about all the wonderful things it does when it splashes. Little white drops run down mom's leg, down the wall and hit the floor. Wow, it's exciting! At two years old, we spill the milk and watch mom's face with a defiant expression and learn about all the exciting things she does with her anger. This really creates excitement! We are angry, but we don't know what to do with it; we don't know how to handle it. We need to learn. So, the best person to learn from is mom, to whom we are closely connected through the symbiosis.[2]

Anger is the primary mechanism used to break out of the dependency relationship with mom. Being responsible for our own feelings, learning to think independently and behaving appropriately are the ways we resolve the symbiosis.

If we are to become fully functioning people who are able to effectively manage our own feeling, thinking and doing, we need mom's help. How our moms handle their anger during these times of obvious challenge provides instruction on how we are to deal with and express anger. When mom appropriately expresses her anger, we experience the consequences for our inappropriate behavior. We learn appropriate expression of anger and, with mom's direction, how to take responsibility for our behavior. This is our first encounter with a social contract. A "social contract" means that we agree to temper our own self-serving behaviors in order to get along with others and still get our needs met. We learn that other people have feelings and thoughts about what we do, which we must take into consideration. We can't just do or say whatever we want in complete disregard for other people. We learn to be aware of other people and learn that others are impacted by what we do.

The social contract provides us with the framework within which to operate in life, enabling us to cooperate and live in harmony with others. We also discover that we are no longer the center of the universe, and this is something else that makes us angry. The world does not revolve around us and will not cater only to our feelings, needs and wants. We must learn that the world is not defined by our feelings. We must also learn that we cannot control parents and the world with our anger, temper tantrums or rebellion. Anger and rebellion must be confronted.

Another revelation for us regarding the social contract is that there are things we must do, whether we want to or not, whether we feel like it or not. You may be shocked to discover some of these same issues surfacing, even now, in your adult life. God will provide the very situation designed to make such dross surface. Two-year-old stuff is alive and well, even in the church, even among Christians. I'm sure you have heard two-year-old banter with a religious twist whenever there is an unpleasant job to do: "Oh, that's not my anointing." "I don't feel led to do that." "God hasn't given me that gift." "I'm not called to that." No one is ever "led" to clean toilets or "anointed" to wash dishes or "called" to change diapers in the nursery. They are not listed among the gifts of the Spirit. They are meant to be the stuff of character building, which leads to dying to self in order to qualify us for the high calling in Christ Jesus (see Eph. 4:1-3).

Toilet Training, Cooperation, Impulse Control, Processing

WHAT? Yes, as improbable as it may seem, these activities are related. Toilet training is a foundational event at this stage of development. Toilet training is an external demand placed on an internal impulse. It is one of the major ways in which issues related to feeling, thinking and doing get worked out concretely. In addition, because toilet training requires the child's willingness and cooperation, it is an important way in which issues surrounding competition, control and cooperation are worked through. Successful toilet training incorporates effective problem solving, self-control, impulse control and the willingness to cooperate into the child's developing personality characteristics. All these attributes are highly significant in establishing the social contract. Without them, the individual is poorly equipped to meet the challenges of future developmental issues and will continue to struggle with two-year-old issues well into adult life. Later on in this chapter, we will discuss, in detail, what happens when a child has been wounded in the toilet-training process.

Discipline

Discipline, appropriately applied, is crucial at this stage of development. It is important for parents to establish basic expectations and daily schedules to which the child must conform. We need confrontation to test our anger and other people's anger, and to learn about limits and consequences for inappropriate behavior. We need to learn to make decisions, which when carried out result in appropriate and acceptable behavior.

Since many people have been wounded by corporal punishment, it would be in order here to briefly discuss disciplinary methods. What are the best methods to accomplish the desired results in a child at this stage? Many parents use corporal punishment by spanking, hitting or, in some way, inflicting physical pain. This, as the belief goes, teaches the child that the consequence for misbehavior is getting hurt. The Christian community generally believes they have been specifically directed by God to spank their children, with reference always being made to Scripture that refers to the "rod" (see Prov. 13:24).

There have been numerous studies conducted on the effectiveness of corporal punishment.[3] The findings of these studies reveal that this method is a most ineffective form of discipline. In many cases it is counterproductive in teaching the child how to be a considerate, loving, responsible adult. Because this is not a parenting book, we do not intend to give an in-depth discussion of disciplinary methods, but we will present what the Lord has revealed to us over our years of ministry. Briefly, spanking a child does not make him/her think or make appropriate and acceptable decisions about future behavior, which is what all of us want from our children. The "rod" in Proverbs does not refer to a literal "beating stick," as many Christians believe. The *NIV Study Bible* note for Proverbs 13:24 states: "Discipline is rooted in love. Rod is probably a figure of speech for discipline of any kind."

Remember, two-year-old children must be taught to think, solve problems and make decisions about behaving appropriately. The most effective discipline is that which promotes and models these behaviors.

Through angry encounters with mom, and appropriate discipline, we come to realize that we are separate from mom and that our feelings are different from hers. We are now becoming responsible for our own feeling, thinking and doing. Parental discipline helps to establish the boundaries between self and others, thereby finally resolving transferring from the symbiosis stage of development. Testing those boundaries helps us to draw the line and establish what is and what is not under our control.

As we receive at this age what we need for healthy growth and development, we are prepared to meet the next stages of life. We have learned to think, solve problems and take responsibility for our behavior. We have established a social contract and have recognized that we are separate from mom; and we are beginning to learn about self-control and self-discipline.

Think back to your childhood: Were you fully equipped to meet the challenges of your next stage of development? Let's now consider what has happened to cause so many people to struggle with two-year-old issues well into adulthood.

Weeds and Roots

Let's return to Michael's story and how the Lord reveals the roots of his pain.

MICHAEL'S STORY (CONTINUED)

Michael never cared about the impact he had on the lives of others . . . until now. His wife's leaving him was the motivation he needed to begin asking God why he had such a problem with his wife and where it all started in his life. Michael had been sitting in the seminar, listening to the teaching about the two-year-old issues. He reported, "When you started talking about adult two-year-olds, controlling mothers and social contracts, I could see myself in everything you said. I am still two years old! I have never committed to anything like a social contract, and my mother wrote the book on control; she is a master at it!" To make matters worse, Michael's father was a rage-aholic who intimidated everyone with his outbursts, everyone except Michael's mother. Michael reflected, "Mom was the only one who kept dad in his place. That was her survival and my protection from him."

The Lord revealed to Michael that even as early as two years old, he began making decisions about how he was going to survive in this world and that someone would have to pay the price for all the control that oppressed him. It was at this moment that the Lord revealed to Michael that he had been controlling, dominating and oppressing others all his life in retaliation for what he had suffered under his mother's domination and control. He had learned well how to survive. The Lord revealed to him that his extremely destructive behavior toward his wife was the main way he was finally getting back at his mother. The person paying the price for his mother's control was Michael's wife. Michael was struck with guilt, grief and agony at this realization. He broke, and a torrent of pain flooded out. As I held him in my arms, his sobs intensified and caught his breath . . . the little child finally could release the grief and pour out the pain buried for so long.

Separating From and Thinking Independently

The birth of independence in separating from mom and learning to think on our own is a very real challenge to survival at this age. We are confronted with a paradox: "If I think and solve problems, will mom still take care of me? Will I be abandoned and left alone?" Fear of not surviving remains the basic issue. If, as a two-year-old, you were convinced that separation into independence and thinking for yourself threatened your mom and might result in her withdrawing care and threatening your survival, you may have decided to avoid thinking at all costs. As a result, you may have lapsed into passivity. This happens in situations with insecure or fearful mothers who are so controlling that they perceive the child's budding independence as a threat to their authority. Perhaps mom was always there pulling you back, doing everything for you, smothering you with constant direction, threats and control, until you could hardly breathe, until the cry of your heart in frustration was, "Mom, I need to do it myself!"

Another opposite but equally destructive scenario is a mother who is so neglectful that becoming independent results in physical harm for the child. Rather than suffering under mom's wrath and anger, as in the example above, physical neglect threatens the child's survival. If this has been your experience, you work at remaining dependent on others so that others will solve problems for you. If you were controlled by mom, you have learned to get what you need by using control. "Not thinking" becomes a control mechanism, a protective device used to deal with the potential dangers in life and to force others to solve your problems.

Anger and the Social Contract

Many people have difficulty dealing with anger because they did not learn how to appropriately express anger at this stage in their development. A two-year-old is skilled at getting mom and dad angry. You yourself felt angry and needed to learn how to deal with it.

When you made mom angry, and she expressed her anger by hitting you, she taught you a lesson. You learned quite well that one expresses anger by hitting or hurting, but you need to wait until you are bigger than the other person.

Another problem that may have occurred during this time if your anger, temper tantrums and rebellion intimidated your parents is that they did not confront you. This resulted in your getting what you wanted, in your learning to control your parents and the world by using anger, rebellion and temper tantrums. Now, as an adult, you feel bound by these same tactics.

Or, perhaps you were overpowered by the anger of your parents. They became very angry with you when you did your two-year-old rebellious routine, becoming more angry and ominous than your little being could handle. They frightened and intimidated you. As a result, you grew up feeling intimidated by authority figures or, as in Michael's case, you learned to intimidate others with your anger to get what you wanted. Either way, the result was an unhealthy, even destructive, lifestyle that cripples you and prevents you from being able to live in harmony with others as God intends.

There are many two-year-olds in grown-up bodies walking around this world. They control through domination, intimidation and manipulation to get what they need and want. They may have learned something about a social contract when they were children, but they have not yet agreed to it or signed it. They are still carrying the wounds they experienced as a two-year-old. These people will pass on this heritage to their descendants.

Toilet Training Wounds

When wounded during toilet training, individuals may struggle not only with issues of shame, but also with problems of self-control, impulse control and cooperation. If toilet training is too harsh or abusive, it adversely affects a child's willingness to cooperate, to think, to solve problems and to incorporate self-control. Instead, they become rebellious and resistant to authority. A "try and make me" attitude toward others, especially toward those in authority, can form. The social contract, which the child had begun to incorporate, will also be negatively affected. Usually, it will become distorted and unhealthy, leading to the kind of person who is unwilling to cooperate readily with others or to submit to those in authority whom God puts in their life. The major adult problem becomes rebellion against God and an unwillingness to submit to His Lordship.

Toilet training too early can also have a negative impact on this stage of development.

MICHAEL'S STORY (CONTINUED)

One of the significant memories the Lord gave Michael was the story he heard his mother tell in which she proudly proclaimed her skills at having toilet trained Michael by the time he was 15 months old, and how she started when he was 12 months old; and even though it took three months, she always boasted of this accomplishment.

As a result of Michael's mother's insistence on toilet training him too early, he never successfully made it through the two-year-old stage of development and never established a social contract. Since, as in his case, early toilet training can only be accomplished by the use of classical conditioning methods—the type of conditioning experimented with by Ivan Pavlov and his famous salivating dogs—the desired behavior is achieved but the child is deprived of the opportunity to confront and accomplish the expectations when developmentally ready. In this way, he or she is deprived of the opportunity to develop effective tools for problem solving.

In the case of toilet training, bowel control is a form of self-control and is one of the building blocks for developing self-discipline as an adult. If children are classically conditioned to perform this activity before they are ready, they are not given the opportunity to deal with the important issues of control and competition/cooperation. They are never really confronted with the opportunity to make a decision, in the strict sense of the word, to cooperate and commit to control their bowels, because they have already been pre-conditioned by external controls.

As mentioned in the previous chapter, being controlled by developmentally inappropriate external demands causes children to relinquish self-control of internal impulses and processes to the control of another person. Basically, children give up the ability to control internal impulses and processes to their parents, thus learning to abandon an internal disciplinary approach to life; they embrace an external disciplinary focus and relinquish the major foundation upon which self-discipline and self-control are built. Such children are often quickly labeled "problem" children and always seem to need parental discipline, correction and punishment. Parents have to monitor and watch them closely or they get into trouble. Is it any wonder they are problem children? They gave up their budding ability to incorporate self-discipline to dominating, controlling parents.

As adults, they may find themselves struggling with self-control and self-discipline. They may do and say things that provoke others to confront and correct them. Many adult Christians find themselves bound by the same sins, which they repeat over and over again. They know they should not do certain things but find it impossible to take control over these patterns of behavior. They keep doing them until someone confronts them and pressures them to change. Obviously, there are other reasons why people continue in the same sins or perform the same inappropriate, hurtful behaviors. Yet, it can often be traced back to having relinquished internal control to an external source.

Many adults—perhaps you are one of them—are held in bondage by this pattern of repeating the same sin over and over again. This lifestyle is most apparent in those who have grown up with controlling parents. (See Appendix B: "Control: Brings Life or Brings Death.")

Discipline Now

Lack of discipline or expectations, inappropriate discipline, harsh discipline enforced with extreme pressure or without having taught the consequences of behavior result in people entering their adult years with many competition/control issues. They have the potential to become a negative, oppositional, rebellious adult who finds it extremely difficult to submit to authority, even to the authority of a living God. They become an uncooperative, self-indulgent person who fears not getting what they need or want in life, so they intimidate, dominate or manipulate to accomplish their goals. Do you know anyone like this?

The Lord desires to set us free from these self-destructive bondages. We need to allow Him to show us the roots of these two-year-old wounds in our lives. He wants to touch these areas, heal our hearts and cleanse our minds. Our God is able to do that.

For the love of Christ compels us (2 Cor. 5:14, *NKJV*).

And God is able to make all grace abound to you, so that in all things at all times, having all that you need, you will abound in every good work (2 Cor. 9:8).

To him who is able to keep you from falling and to present you before his glorious presence without fault and with great joy—to the only God, our Savior be glory, majesty, power and authority, through Jesus Christ our Lord, before all ages, now and forevermore! Amen (Jude 24-25).

Father God's Intervention

Once more, the only way this cycle will ever be broken is to recognize it, take responsibility for the wounds in our lives and let the Lord touch these two-year-old issues and heal them. When we become free, we can then pass this freedom on as an inheritance to future generations.

MICHAEL'S STORY (CONTINUED)

As we sat together, I prayed and asked the Lord to reveal Himself to Michael. A series of incidents when he was two to three years old replayed through his memory, incidents where he and his mother were locked in battles over who was going to get their way, Mom or Michael. In each situation where the control was oppressive, the Lord revealed Himself and protected Michael from the attack of the spirit of control. In situations where Michael was the one rebelling and controlling, the Lord again intervened to confront Michael and parent him, providing the correction and setting the boundaries he needed for security. In each memory, Michael experienced himself giving up control to the Lord and submitting to the Lord's corrective discipline. The Lord brought him through situation after situation for over an hour and revealed Himself in each memory, setting Michael more and more free of layers of "stuff." When no more memories came, Michael prayed to break the power of the spirit of control in his life, in the generations and over his wife. He repented and asked Father God to father him and guide him in situations where he would automatically tend to move into control. Another major result of this prayer time was that Michael committed to sign and live by a social contract, symbolically, of course.

Over the past several years, it has not been easy for Michael. Yet, he is committed to work out what the Lord has worked into his heart. Michael's wife has since returned. He is dramatically different in his behavior toward her and others. He still slips back into control now and then, but as soon as he recognizes it, he immediately deals with it and takes personal responsibility for his behavior. Another radical change is that Michael is now sensitive toward others and very much aware of the impact he has on them. He is no longer the prideful, self-seeking controller he used to be. He has moved on to pursue greater maturity.

There are many of us who have been wounded as Michael was. For some of us the wounding is more extreme; for others it is less extreme. No matter how deep your past wounds are, the Lord will walk through those experiences with you again and reveal the Father's intention for that time in your life. In His presence you will find the healing and the freedom you long for. The lies and bondages have no more power. The Truth Himself sets you free.

Truth: Facing the Pain

Although it is often viewed in a positive light, at the very least control is a counterfeit power. It relies on human strength, or "the arm of flesh," as the Bible calls it. At its very worst, control is a spirit that influences words and actions and challenges the lordship of Christ. In truth, when exercised over people, control is very destructive. Control hinders independence, thinking and problem solving and encourages inordinate dependence on authority. It breeds competition and conflict. A person wounded by control can grow up to be controlling, rebellious, competitive to a fault, or passive, overly adaptive and overly submissive.

Revelation: Revisiting the Scene

Sometimes denial and familiarity can block us from seeing the truth. We need the Holy Spirit to break through, search our hearts and shine His light of revelation. Ask Him to show you the roots of any destruction in this time of your life. You need not face it alone: Jesus will be there to walk through that time again with you; just ask Him to reveal His presence.

Redemption: Healing and Deliverance

If we receive what we need at this stage of our development, we become independent, able to think and solve problems and to take personal responsibility for our behavior. But, if not, we need healing and freedom from the bondages that arrested our development. Control is a counterfeit of godly discipline. Discipline is needed now to learn how to submit to proper authority in a healthy way. The Lord will uproot the destructive effects of oppressive or negligent parenting and restore the healthy limits and boundaries we need for security and healthy self-discipline in our lives.

Restoration: The Planting of the Lord

The Lord wants to restore you and provide what you needed to become a separate person at this two-year-old stage. He will again establish the boundaries you need for security and will supernaturally impart into your life the foundation necessary for self-discipline.

Reparenting: Father God, "Father" Us

Learning to submit to the Lordship of Jesus is a progressive pursuit, but it is impossible without a healthy resolution of our two-year-old stuff. Once healed and restored, the daily discipline of seeking the Lord, listening to Him and obeying Him will strengthen self-discipline and healthy submission to the proper authority God has placed over us for our good.

THE FATHER'S HEALING PROCESS:
STEPS TO HEALING, FREEDOM AND RESTORATION

Healing

1. Identify the adult problems—behaviors and attitudes—that apply to you. (See Tables 4A/4B: Healthy/Unhealthy Development.)

2. Ask the Holy Spirit to reveal the root cause of each problem—whatever happened to you as a two-year-old that caused a wounding in your life and allowed the problem to take root. The Holy Spirit may reveal this to you in the form of a memory, picture, impression, thought, awareness, or some other way of "knowing" (see Luke 8:17).

3. Ask Jesus to reveal His presence there with you. The presence of the Lord changes everything (see Ps. 31:14-15; Heb. 13:5-6,8).

4. Tell Jesus what you are feeling and thinking in this time, place or experience. Listen to His response (see Pss. 88:1; 91:14-16).

5. Ask Jesus to reveal what the Father intended for this time of your life. Jesus comes to show us the Father. Allow the Lord to minister to you; rest in Him and take time to receive what you need. He comes to care for your developmental needs, to heal you, to redeem all that was lost to you and to restore you to be all He created you to be (see Jer. 29:11; Matt. 15:13).

Freedom

6. In the name of Jesus, break the power of the lie that was planted in your heart from the wound and ask the Father to uproot it.

Embrace the truth—the Word of God that has the power to set you free. Proclaim the promises in God's Word that are His answers to your need (see Matt. 15:13; John 8:31-32; 2 Cor. 1:20).

7. Identify any patterns of sin, bondages, curses that passed from generation to generation in your family. Break any generational curses, if necessary. (See also Appendix A: Generational Curses.) Forgive your parents and all those who wounded you (see Matt. 6:14; Gal. 3:13-14).

8. Take authority in Jesus' name over any demonic oppression or influences in your life that the Lord has revealed. In the name and authority of Jesus, command them to leave in Jesus' name (see Luke 10:19; Jas. 4:7).

Restoration

9. Receive Father God as your eternal Father and receive your inheritance of life through Christ Jesus. Seek the Father each day and ask Him to father you (see John 10:10; Heb. 12:10).

10. Ask the Holy Spirit to teach you how to walk in your "newness of life." Commit to listen to and obey the Holy Spirit, and begin to put God's Word into action in your life (see John 14:26; 16:13; Phil. 2:12-13).

Table 4A: Healthy Development

Stage of Life	Significant Issues	Developmental Task (needed for healthy development)	Adult Manifestation
2 Years	Independence/ thinking	Initial breaking of symbiosis	Considerate of others
	Anger, opposition, rebellion	Establish separateness	Think effectively/ problem solver
	Establish social contract	Incorporate social contract	Submit to rightful authority

Table 4A: Healthy Development (continued)

Stage of Life	Significant Issues	Developmental Task (needed for healthy development)	Adult Manifestation
2 Years	Separation, control Cooperation vs. competition	Learn limits and boundaries Accept discipline Learn cooperation Develop cause-and-effect thinking	Self-disciplined, cooperative Synergistic* relationships Submit to the Lordship of Jesus Cooperate with the Holy Spirit

* **Synergy:** The working together of two (or more) to produce an effect greater than the sum of the individual effects.

Table 4B: Unhealthy Development

Stage of Life	Significant Issues	Developmental Task (needed for healthy development)	Adult Manifestation
2 Years	Independence/ thinking Anger/ opposition rebellion social contract Separation Control Cooperation vs. competition	No discipline or expectations Consequences of behavior not taught Expectations too high or enforced with extreme pressure Parents demand dependency/ submission to control Anger not confronted or not dealt with effectively	Inconsiderate of others Lack self-discipline Oppositional/ competitive/ controlling Symbiotic in relationships Self-centered Difficulty thinking effectively and problem solving

Table 4B: Unhealthy Development (continued)

Stage of Life	Significant Issues	Developmental Task (needed for healthy development)	Adult Manifestation
2 Years		Control issues not confronted Inappropriate modeling of anger by parent No clear boundaries/ limits	Anger that discounts others Lack social contract Oppose/resist the Holy Spirit

IDENTITY

Three to Five Years of Age

TOM'S STORY

Tom was just five years old when his father returned from the war a broken man. During his father's absence, Tom's mother was lonely and very frightened about the future. She found her only joy was in raising her children, especially Tom, who was her favorite. As her favorite, Tom was given special attention, sometimes in ways that confused him. A knot tightened in his stomach whenever she pulled him close to her. At times, when his mother was especially frightened and lonely, she would have Tom sleep beside her for comfort. Tom felt quite uncomfortable during these times.

Between the ages of three and five, children learn to identify social roles and conceptualize what the world is about. What is seen is done; what is heard is repeated. It is time to incorporate identity, to discover what it means to be male or female. The family, social setting and culture all play an important role in shaping the development of young children of this age. Mother and father are particularly significant role models.[1]

Adult Problems

To know your identity is to know the truth of who you are and who you were created to be. Adult problems affecting identity can have a devastating effect on our ability to recognize and fulfill our destiny. If we don't know who we are, how can we be who God intended us to be in this world and fulfill our purpose? In considering the importance of this stage of development, it is critical to recognize the adult problems that can take root during this time. Some of the most common struggles include: sex-role confusion, over-adaptation, fears and phobias, fantasies without action, social ineptitude, rituals/compulsive behaviors, self-righteous/legalistic behaviors, distorted perceptions.

TOM'S STORY (CONTINUED)

Tom is a likable guy. He is well thought of by everyone in town, outside his home. Yet, deep inside, Tom was tormented by an oppressive sense of shame. He had struggled all his life with sexual identity problems and was addicted to sexually explicit movies and porn on the Internet. Sexual relations with his wife had taken on more perverted patterns as the addiction tightened its grip. Tom and his wife had sought counseling with some results. Yet, the main issues of deep shame, sexual addiction, sexual perversion and a lack of emotional closeness had not been touched.

Tom is not alone. Sex-role confusion is more common than you might think. Many people struggle with insecurity in their identity as a man or a woman. The blurring of sex-role differences in today's culture does not help the situation. Sex-role confusion does not mean a person is homosexual but, rather, is not completely comfortable and secure in knowing how to *be* and behave in appropriate ways for his or her sexual identity. (Homosexuality is a much more severe identity crisis, related to many other influences that will be discussed in a later chapter.)

Do you feel compelled by others to say and do what you perceive they expect of you? Would you describe yourself as socially inept or an introvert conversationally? Are you comfortable with the fact that God created you a male or female, or do you struggle with your identity? Do you experience problems in the area of sex? Have you been tormented by fear for as long as you can remember? If you answered "yes" to any of the above questions, it's likely that the roots of such issues can be traced back to the time when you were three to five years old.

To get a better understanding of the roots of these problems, let's revisit the tender ages of three to five, and walk through our development again.

Developmental Process

Three Years Old

We discovered in the previous chapter that at two years old a social contract is established. A great deal of information gathering is necessary in order to put this contract to work. At three years old, what we see, we do; and what we hear, we say. If it's okay for mom and dad, it's okay for me. It's likely that we will say and do things learned from adults at the most inappropriate times, much to the chagrin of our parents. Even so, parents love this age. They enjoy the welcome relief from the previous year's time of testing and opposition. Three-year-olds are very helpful, doing things for their parents, even without being asked. They are lovable, helpful and considerate.

Our insatiable drive for information motivates parents to consult the encyclopedia to answer the consistently voiced and ever-present question, "Why?" God gives all three-year-olds a one-word gift: "Why?" Parents must work hard, at times, not to use the two-word response, "BE QUIET!" which can emerge out of frustration after the numerous whys. Do parents ever run out of answers? YES!

We are very perceptive now. Nothing seems to escape our awareness. We are collecting information about the world, and it's important that we receive accurate information without being ridiculed, teased or made fun of. We are learning what people will and will not respond to. As much as we need to learn socially appropriate behavior, we also need to learn conversational etiquette: when it's okay to talk and when we must be polite and remain silent; what is appropriate to say and what is not appropriate to say.

We experience our feelings and those of others around us and we must learn to integrate these feelings with what's happening in our environment. Our parents need to spend some time helping us label feelings: "This is happy," "This is sad," "This is angry," and so on. In this way, we begin to understand the responses we, and others, have to the events happening around us. At this age, we develop strong connections between feeling, thinking and doing. We test thoughts and perceptions in order to develop a foundational understanding of what it means to function socially as a human being.

Four Years Old

By the time we are four years old, being well behaved becomes a major concern. We desire to be a good child for our parents. We've been collecting information for a whole year. The more we learn about the world, the more we begin to wonder if we will be good enough to make it in this world.

Fear Happens

Have you ever noticed how, at four years old, children seem to get into fear? They begin to have nightmares and talk about scary events and ghosts. They want you to read them stories of Jesus' delivering people of demons. This is the age of the nightlight because nighttime is dark and scary. As already mentioned, being well behaved is important for a four-year-old. Often, four-year-olds feel like they will not be good enough to make it in the world, and so they discover a mechanism to make themselves behave: they scare themselves. For example, if people are overwhelmed with fear, they report being *frozen* with fear, not able to move. If you don't move, you can't behave badly. This is the extreme case, but you get the idea. Fear then becomes the self-imposed control mechanism to accomplish the goal of good behavior.

At this age, we need consistent, structured discipline. The more we must control our own behavior without parental involvement, the more fear we will generate to accomplish this. The issue becomes one of parenting. The more structured and consistent the parents are in their discipline, the less the child will adopt fear. We need to know that our parents will be there to help us be the good child we desire to be. Yet, the more parents are inconsistent in their discipline or do not provide enough parental structure for our needs, the greater will be our fear. This is a time when we become susceptible to a spirit of fear taking hold and controlling us for the rest of our life. This might not make much sense to an adult, but it makes perfect sense to a four-year-old.

If parents provided us with consistency and structure and did not reinforce the fear by using it against us as a disciplinary tool, then we were well prepared to meet the five-year-old issues with confidence and strength.

Five Years Old

By the time we are five years old we have established confidence in what is right and wrong. We know what is supposed to be done, but we will have trouble doing it. We will need to practice the "doing," which is what the six- to twelve-year-old stage of development is all about.

Self-righteous

This is a very self-righteous age. We see everything as black or white, right or wrong. If you want to see what legalism looks like in its purest form, observe five-year-olds. There is little grace in a child of this age. Parents will need to be perfect in all their ways or the five-year-old will be there to remind them when they are not.

At this stage of development we become strongly acculturated. We now incorporate many of the family standards, values and mores, as well as receive a great deal of information about the roles that males and females play in the family, the culture and the world. How do males and females fit into the family structure? How do males relate to other males and females? How do females relate to other females and males? We receive much training in these roles by observing and interacting with mother and father. Father becomes the major role model for sons, and mother becomes the major role model for daughters. Both parents give important information about what role we are to occupy as an adult in the family structure and society. Because social right and wrong is a major focus now, any time we observe anyone transcending what is socially acceptable, it will frighten us and threaten our developing sense of righteousness. When father exuberantly drives faster than is allowed, we will inform him of his sin.

I can remember a time when Todd, our son, was five years old and I took him to the market. A new shipment of grapes had just arrived and was out on the counter for sale. I decided to taste a grape to see if they were sweet before I bought some. I put one in my mouth and began to chew it. Shocked by what I had done, Todd shouted at the top of his voice, "Daddy, Daddy, spit that out!" Startled, I spat out the chewed grape. I thought there was something terribly wrong with the grape. I said, "What, son?" With tears in his eyes, Todd said, "You're going to go to jail. You stole a grape." Legally, I had stolen a grape. The right thing would have been to allow Todd to see me ask permission to taste a grape before I did so. I could have avoided the embarrassment I felt as the people around me looked with disapproval at the thief in their midst. But, more importantly, I could have spared my son the shock he experienced when his sense of righteousness was affronted.

Many children become wounded in their sense of righteousness at this age, because significant adults in their lives do things that are inconsistent with their learning about what is right and appropriate, behaviorally and socially.

A Time to Pray

Because we have no trouble believing in God at this age, it is a good time to learn how to pray. I believe God really enjoys answering the prayers of five-year-olds. They can be formidable prayer warriors who seem to get their prayers answered with very little delay on God's part. They have no trouble believing God. They know that if He said it, He will do it. Their faith can, at times, far surpass the faith of many adults.

A father told me about a prayer time he had with his five-year-old. The father came home from work with a terrible cold. His nose was all stuffed up and he could hardly breathe through it. He sat down on the couch to rest. His son, seeing his father in great discomfort, walked over and asked if he could pray for him. The father, knowing five-year-olds get their prayers answered, said, "Yes, son, please pray for me." The son placed one hand on his father's nose, and with the other hand raised toward heaven, he spoke in the best prayer warrior voice he could generate, "Heal it . . . or take it, Lord!" The father quickly responded, "Hold on . . . I like my nose!"

The father's warning to me was, "Be careful *how* you teach your five-year-old to pray."

Secure Sex-Role Identity

By the end of these three years of development, we have a good understanding of our identity. We have incorporated the "shoulds" and "should-nots" from home and the society in which we live.[2] Armed with socially appropriate behavior, a secure identity and parent-instilled problem-solving structures, we are well equipped to experience and actively be involved in the next stage of childhood, six to twelve years, and *active* it is.

Let's now look at some of the wounds that can occur during the ages of three to five.

Weeds and Roots

Why?!

At three years old, we enjoy exercising our newfound verbal abilities. We talk a lot, ask a lot of questions and are very sensitive to our parents' needs.

Adults who feel socially inept or uncomfortable, and fear asking questions, especially of authority figures, will often find the root cause back at three years old. Such feelings often arise when children feel pressured to stop talking by parents who are frustrated with constant conversation and questions. This is when self-esteem can be negatively affected and children begin to feel something is wrong with them. This sense of shame can then form the foundation for the belief that they are not significant, they have nothing important to say and they have no right to assert themselves verbally. Living with such bondage may create a pattern in later life whereby they frequently make assumptions about what people mean, expect or want from them, without being totally sure. They consequently find themselves making errors of judgment, resulting in mistakes that cause problems for themselves and others.

People who feel teased or ridiculed during this time of information gathering may find themselves having problems being serious about and focusing on learning new things, and may feel insecure in their perceptions of reality. Also, they may experience a great deal of skepticism when given new information, because they don't trust the person who has provided it.

Fear

We have met many adults who have experienced a pervasive sense of fear nearly all their lives. These people had incorporated a spirit of fear at the time when they were most susceptible to it, when they were four years old.

SUSAN'S STORY

Susan's request for prayer was motivated by bondage to fear. This fear was robbing her of her joy and freedom in life. During prayer, the Lord revealed to Susan a time when she was four years old and she was riding her little three-wheel bike on the upstairs back porch of her home. Her younger brother began swiftly crawling toward the stairs, which led down to the ground floor. Susan raced over with her bike to try to put herself between her brother and the stairs before he toppled down them. She just made it in time, but in the process she managed to run over his little hand, and he began screaming. Susan was standing with her legs straddling either side of the bike at the edge of the top step. In fear, anger and frustration, her mother came running over, and without asking what had happened, she hit Susan for hurting her brother.

When Susan was hit, she lost her balance and tumbled head over heels, bike and all, down the stairs. Susan landed on the ground floor with a broken arm. She remembers screaming in fear and pain, and her mother running down the stairs crying out, "Oh, Susan, I'm sorry . . . oh, Susan, I'm so sorry!" By this time the intense fear evoked by the situation had created an opening for a spirit of fear in her life. Susan incorporated this fear and it remained as a pervasive controlling force up until the present time.

As we sat praying, we asked the Lord to reveal Himself in that memory. Susan experienced the Lord come to her, pick her up and console and comfort her. At that moment, she felt an amazing peace come over her and experienced a dramatic release as all fear vanished from her mind. After a few moments, Susan prayed to forgive her mom, and she took authority over the spirit of fear. She renounced this fear and proclaimed: "For God has not given us a spirit of fear " (2 Tim. 1:7, *NKJV*). Susan was free. After 23 years of being controlled by fear, she was free!

There are many people like Susan who, at four years of age, incorporated a spirit of fear into their being. If fear is a problem in your life, it could be the result of a traumatic event you suffered at this age.

In some cases the problem gets compounded by adults who actually use fear as a means of disciplining.

FRANK'S STORY

Frank was staying with his aunt and uncle for several weeks. One day, Frank's aunt saw him hiding behind the bushes, watching the men pick up the trash. Frank was obviously afraid of these men, and his aunt recognized it. Later, when Frank was into some mischief, giving his aunt a hard time, she shouted at him, "If you don't behave, I will call those garbage men to take you away!" That was all Frank needed. He stopped his misbehaving. But every night for 20 years thereafter, Frank had horrible, frightening nightmares of running in panic from men who were coming in garbage trucks to take him away. This was a big price to pay for a quick-fix disciplinary technique. Frank received ministry and was set free of the fear.

Fear will stop misbehavior, but the price in terms of the enduring negative repercussions is too high. Was your four-year-old fear used against you because your parents knew no other way to discipline your behavior? Any abuse—whether emotional, physical or sexual—is deeply wounding during this stage of development. The heightened sensitivity to sexual identity and fear makes us more vulnerable to bondages and wounds taking root, and the effects can be devastating throughout childhood and into adult life.

Whatever happened to you when you were at this age, the Lord can easily and swiftly set you free now. He is no respecter of persons (see Acts 10:34). What He did for Susan, Frank and many others, He will do for you.

The Bondage of Self-righteousness

Do you find yourself compelled and driven to "defend the faith," to take a stand for righteousness, to identify with a cause or to correct those who are in error? The key words here are "compelled and driven." All healthy adults need to stand for their faith, to be righteous in their dealings with others, and to be accurate and truthful in word and deed. Yet, adults who were wounded in their sense of righteousness when they were five years old may later find themselves with a driving, compelling need to correct people they perceive as unrighteous.

EDWARD'S STORY

Edward would get furious when someone said or did something that was socially unacceptable or incorrect. He became even angrier if a religious leader said or did something he perceived as unrighteous by God's standards. Edward operated by the law. His self-righteous attitude got him into trouble many times, especially with his pastor. Many times he was told he was too fanatical and that he had a religious spirit, to which he reacted with "holy anger."

Edward had a very difficult time extending grace to others when he believed they were wrong. He was unable to walk away from what he perceived as obvious unrighteousness.

During prayer, the Lord revealed to Edward that when he was five years old, the time when children are most sensitive to issues of righteousness, he consistently witnessed his father committing obvious unrighteous and inappropriate acts. He witnessed his father hitting his mother, stealing from stores, lying to people when Edward knew the real truth. He clearly remembered his father correcting him and punishing him for the very things he witnessed his father doing. Edward was wounded in his sense of righteousness. He made a decision at five years old that he would correct anyone he perceived was acting unrighteously.

After ministry, prayer and the Lord's intervention in many of Edward's five-year-old memories with his father, he was systematically set free. He renounced the decision he had made to be the defender of righteousness and gave the responsibility back to Jesus, where it belongs. He asked the Lord to give him a revelation of His grace and mercy, as he already knew about godly discipline and fear.

As the Lord brings to mind three-, four- and five-year-old childhood memories, His purpose is to revisit them with you and heal you of wounds you may have received. The Lord will set you free of the issues that are bondages and obstacles to growth and maturity in Him. Don't allow five-year-old self-righteousness, four-year-old fear or three-year-old shame and inadequacy hold you back from allowing the Lord to touch these areas in your life. Healing is a free gift from God to you.

Sex-Role Confusion

Let's now look at the significant roots of the wounds that the Lord revealed to Tom. During the two hours we were together, Tom offered the following background information:

Tom was the oldest of three children, and the only boy. Tom's father was away at war during his first few years of life. The closeness that had developed between Tom and his mother became even more uncomfortable when Tom's father came home from the war. Tom's father—depressed, withdrawn and struggling with drug addiction—was incapable of attending to his wife's emotional needs. Tom, at five years old, began to feel quite embarrassed by his mother's attentions. He remembered nights when his father was not home and his mother would ask him to sit close to her on the couch. By the time he was six years old, he felt enormous shame. He remembers the question was always in his mind, "Why do I feel so badly? Mom needs me." He remembers praying and asking God to bring his father home so he could go to bed, not wanting to abandon his mother.

As we began to pray, the Lord revealed significant roots to Tom's adult problems.

Since Tom's father was unavailable to meet his wife's emotional needs for companionship and support as a husband normally does, she subconsciously turned to Tom for the emotional support she lacked. Tom became a surrogate husband for his mother. As well as receiving healthy nurture from his mother, Tom was being required to take her adult emotional needs on board. This mixture was a potent, destructive concoction that resulted in throwing Tom into emotional and sex-role confusion.

Because this occurred at the age when sex-role identity is a significant developmental issue, Tom became susceptible to sex-role confusion, which created a perversion in Tom's attitudes about sex and sexual activity. Although there was nothing of a physical sexual nature in his mother's interaction with him, this emotional confusion was the root of the intense shame Tom was experiencing.

Such a situation in families can be considered "emotional incest." Tom's mother certainly did not intend this to occur in her relationship with her son; nevertheless, when a wife's emotional needs for intimacy with her husband remain unmet, they can get mixed up with her normal emotional interactions with her children.

Tom also recognized that he had made a conscious decision to care for his mother and always be there for her, no matter what the cost. This decision was the root cause of why Tom and his wife had never been emotionally close to each other, which in turn was creating the same situation for Tom's wife that his mother had experienced with her husband. Tom's wife was turning to their oldest son for the satisfaction of her emotional needs in the same way that Tom's mom had turned to him. The problem was being passed on from father to son. Tom was shocked to recognize how such perversion and destruction could be handed from one generation to the next. (For more on this, see Appendix A.)

Tom is just one of many people we have met who have suffered with this problem, which appears to be more prevalent in some cultures than others. The attack on sexual identity through this wounding is ruthless. Furthermore, we have found that such problems are not male-specific.

Women experience similar distortion and perversion in their relationships with their mothers. When there is no son in the family, or the son does not respond to his mother's emotional needs, the mother may take a daughter as a "surrogate spouse." If this occurs when she is between three and five years old, the sex-role confusion may have the added component of animosity or hatred toward men and susceptibility toward homosexual abuses from women. Even though there is no overt physical sexual abuse, the emotional sexual abuse is deeply wounding to sexual identity.

When this unhealthy connection happens between a father and daughter, she grows up to disrespect men, often manipulating them through seductive behavior to validate her belief that they are weak and easily controlled. The fact that children forced into this role experience power over the parent for whom they are emotionally caring produces a love/hate dynamic in the relationship. On the one hand, they hate being able to control the parent; on the other hand, they like the special favor and power they are able to exert. When a father puts a daughter into this position, it creates a sense of competition between mother and daughter, which later displaces to women in general.

In all these cases, there will be problems in a future marriage relationship. When we are bonded wrongly to a parent, then our spouse is immediately displaced from his/her rightful position beside us. The perverted connection needs to be broken so that our wounds can be healed.

MARIA'S STORY

Maria is a stunning young woman. Her beauty and charm would have been lovely, had they not been distorted. Maria was compulsively seductive. Her self-hatred and shame had brought her to the brink of suicide more than once. But this time she was finally ready to face the pain in her life. When she asked the Holy Spirit to reveal the root of her compulsion, a clear memory came into focus. Maria was her father's favorite, often displacing her mother in his affections and attention. When she was about five years old, her father disciplined her for misbehaving. She was angry and gave her father the silent treatment for several hours. Finally, unable to bear her rejection of him, her father came weeping and begging her to speak to him. She knew from that point on that she was in control of her father. She hated his weakness but at the same time loved the power she had.

Now as an adult, she played out the same scenario with men in authority. Only now she used seduction to manipulate them and had brought many men down in moral failure, proving her belief. She said she targeted men who were full of pride, pretending to be strong when really they were weak.

Maria could not bear the pain of her shame and guilt anymore. She repented and asked the Lord to reveal His presence to her in that early time. He came to release her from the overwhelming neediness of her father and set her free to be a little girl. Jesus took her place and cared for her father. Jesus then broke the ungodly connection between her and her father. Maria also broke the unhealthy connection to her father, in Jesus' name, and forgave her father. She prayed to break the generational curses of a man-hating spirit, a spirit of perversion, abuse, self-destruction and suicide. She left these bondages at the cross and rose to new life.[3] And Maria asked Jesus to restore to her a healthy view of men. She is learning to be the lovely woman God made her to be.

Maria's perverted bonding with her father distorted her identity as a woman. Because of her broken identity, she was vulnerable to the influence of the enemy. He was destroying her as well as the men she seduced. Jesus understands our pain and bondage. He is always ready to forgive us, heal us, set us free and restore us.

Father God's Intervention
TOM'S STORY (CONTINUED)

The time of prayer with Tom was emotional and dynamic. We asked the Lord to show Tom what had been significant in his childhood. Within moments the Lord revealed a time when Tom was lying in his bed with his mother lying next to him, kissing him goodnight. He felt extreme shame, fear and revulsion. The Lord revealed that this particular incident occurred at a time when his mom's emotional needs were at an extremely high level. This was also the moment when Tom made the decision to always take care of his mom. The connection was made and the torment began, which Tom had lived with all his life.

We asked the Lord to reveal Himself in this memory. Tom reported, "Jesus is walking into my room. He's motioning to my mom to get off my bed and to come to Him. My mom is going to Jesus. He's taking my mom in His arms and she's crying. Jesus is taking care of my mom Himself. Jesus speaks to my mom as He holds her. Then Jesus turns to me and tells me that He will care for my mom. That it is not my responsibility. I feel the shame and fear go. I'm free!"

Tom then prayed to break all unhealthy emotional, sexual and symbiotic connections between him and his mother—every tie, connection and attachment in his spirit, mind, will and emotions. Tom broke the power of perversion, confusion and shame in his life. He forgave his mom and asked the Lord to forgive her for what she did. He asked the Lord to forgive him for taking on responsibility for his mom when it really belonged to Jesus. Tom renounced the decision to always take care of his mom and always remain emotionally tied to her so she could get her needs met. He prayed to finally leave his mom, break the bondage with her and family, to cleave to his wife and to work at becoming one flesh with her (see Gen. 2:24). He then prayed to receive his wife by his side in her rightful place as wife, friend and lover. Tom was finally free to be the husband he wanted to be.

Your identity is critical to your future. If you don't know who you are, how can you lay hold of your rightful inheritance? If you don't know who you are created to be, how can you fulfill your purpose and destiny? The Father wants to heal you and restore what was lost. He wants to set you free.

Truth: Facing the Pain

Pain can only continue to hurt us if it remains hidden. When we bring it into the light and seek the Lord for healing, He will set us free. Let Jesus show you what He wants to deal with in your life from the ages of three to five years old. These formative years are critical to your personal identity and your social/cultural identity.

Revelation: Revisiting the Scene

The Holy Spirit knows the root of your pain. Allow Him to bring to your attention anything that happened in your life at this stage of development that still hinders you today. He may give you a picture, a memory, an impression, an awareness or some other way of "knowing." There is no need to fear. What the Lord reveals, He heals. The Holy Spirit knows just what we need to know in order to be set free.

JEN'S STORY

Jen had been oppressed by fear for as long as she could remember. She was afraid to go out at night. She was afraid to be alone at night. The fear grew worse as the years passed. When she came for ministry, we asked the Holy Spirit to reveal the root of her fear. She saw herself in a dark place when she was about four years old, and she heard a struggle and her mother crying, but she could not see clearly what was happening. She felt the fear come over her. We prayed and asked Jesus to reveal Himself in the picture. Jen could not see Him and began to panic. Then the Lord said, "Tell Jen to take a deep breath and tell you what she smells." When she took a deep breath, she said, "I smell clean sheets!" Jesus told her, "I am here, holding you close to My shoulder. This is not for you to see." Suddenly the realization came. "I smell Jesus!" Jen blurted, and immediately the fear lifted. Jen commanded the fear to leave in Jesus' name, and it did, never to return.

Redemption: Healing and Deliverance

In this time of development we may be wounded more by our perceptions of reality than by what actually happened. However, the wounds are just as real and need to be healed. Parents often do not know how to provide what we need for healthy development, and we are left with unmet needs. Only Jesus can meet those needs now. Ask Him to reveal His presence in those times of need and fill up your empty places inside.

Restoration: The Planting of the Lord

The Father wants to redeem what was lost at this time in your life. He will supernaturally impart into your being the truth of your identity as a free child of the living God. He will answer all your "whys." He will even answer the hard questions harbored in your heart. Only Father God can quiet your anxious heart—He alone gives the peace that passes understanding. He will invite you to embrace your true identity as a man or woman, according to His perfect plan for your life. His perfect love will cast out all fear and give you love, power and a strong mind.

Reparenting: Father God, "Father" Me

Each day the Father waits for you to seek Him again, to hear from His heart, to receive all that He wants to teach you about His ways. He wants to teach you, train you, correct you, nurture you—for your good—so that you might share in His holiness (see Heb. 12:10).

THE FATHER'S HEALING PROCESS:
STEPS TO HEALING, FREEDOM AND RESTORATION

Healing

1. Identify the adult problems—behaviors and attitudes that apply to you. (See Tables 5A/5B: Healthy/Unhealthy Development.)

2. Ask the Holy Spirit to reveal the root cause of each problem—whatever happened to you between the ages of three and five that caused a wounding in your life and allowed the problem to take root. The Holy Spirit may reveal this to you in the form of a memory, a picture, an impression, a thought, an awareness or some other way of "knowing" (see Luke 8:17).

3. Ask Jesus to reveal His presence there with you. The Lord's presence changes everything (see Pss. 31:14-16; 139:1-12; Heb. 13:5-6,8).

4. Tell Jesus what you are feeling and thinking in this time, place or experience. Listen to His response (see Pss. 88:1; 91:14-16).

5. Ask Jesus to reveal what the Father intended for this time of your life. Jesus comes to show us the Father. Allow the Lord to minister to you; rest in Him and take time to receive what you need. He comes to care for your developmental needs, to heal you, to redeem all that was lost to you and to restore you to be all He created you to be (see Jer. 29:11; Matt. 15:13).

Freedom

6. In the name of Jesus, break the power of the lie that was planted in your heart from the wound and ask the Father to uproot it. Embrace the truth—the Word of God—that has the power to set you free. Proclaim the promises in God's Word that are His answers to your need (see Matt. 15:13; John 8:31-32; 2 Cor. 1:20).

7. Identify any patterns of sin, bondages or curses that passed from generation to generation in your family. Break any generational curses, if necessary. (See also Appendix A: Generational Curses.) Forgive your parents and all those who wounded you (see Matt. 6:14; Gal. 3:13-14).

8. Take authority in Jesus' name over any demonic oppression or influences in your life that the Lord has revealed. In the name of Jesus and His authority, command them to leave (see Luke 10:19; Jas. 4:7).

Restoration

9. Receive Father God as your eternal Father and receive your inheritance of life through Christ Jesus. Seek the Father each day and ask Him to father you (see John 10:10; Heb. 12:10).

10. Ask the Holy Spirit to teach you how to walk in your "newness of life." Commit to listen to and obey the Holy Spirit, and begin to put God's Word into action in your life (see John 14:26; 16:13; Phil. 2:12-13).

Table 5A: Healthy Development

Stage of Life	Significant Issues	Developmental Task (needed for healthy development)	Adult Manifestation
3 Years to 5 Years	Identity: how to fit in	Identify with healthy role model	Acceptance of identity
	Sex-role identification	Appropriate answers to "why?"	Healthy sex-role identity
	Personal effect on relationships	Information seeking encouraged	Secure in social situations
	Information gathering	Connections made between feeling and thinking	Strong connections of feeling, thinking and problem solving
	Learn social and conversational skills	Learn to define and label feelings	Social and conversational appropriateness
	Acculturation	Appropriate conversational and social behavior learned	Unshakable identity in Christ
		Incorporate cultural identity	

Table 5B: Unhealthy Development

Stage of Life	Significant Issues	Developmental Task (needed for healthy development)	Adult Manifestation
3 Years to 5 Years	Identity: how to fit in	Lack of healthy role models	Overly adaptive
	Sex-role identification	Emotional/ physical/ sexual abuse	Self-righteous/ legalistic
	Personal effect on relationships	Inconsistent, unstructured parenting	Sex-role confusion
	Information gathering	Parenting excludes child's thinking	Inept in social situations
	Social and conversational skills	Fear reinforced or used against child	Poor connections between feeling, thinking, doing/ problem solving
	Acculturation	Socially appropriate behavior not taught	Lack social and conversational skills
		Sense of righteousness affronted	Rejection of identity
			Fear used to motivate self
			Oppressed by fear of man
			Oppressed by spirit of fear
			Tenuous identity in Christ

GIFTS AND CALLINGS

Six to Twelve Years of Age

MARKUS'S STORY

Markus had just come home from school; he was in the kitchen when the doorbell rang. His mother answered the door. It was a police officer bringing the tragic news that Markus's father had just been killed in an auto accident. His mother collapsed in shock, disbelief and grief. Markus, stunned, ran to his mom. They held on to each other as the reality slowly sank in.

What a tragedy for a nine-year-old child to be confronted with during this very formative time of his life.

This is the stage of life—ages six to twelve—when children are concentrating on developing the skills necessary to survive in the world independently. This is the time when they are learning how to be effective and are developing the confidence that "I can do it." They are developing a code of values and a strong moral foundation and will work on being skillful in all areas, primarily learning how to learn. *Doing* is emphasized, with *feelings* relegated to a low priority. Healthy competition and skills testing are paramount now.[1]

Adult Problems

Are you inflexible, impatient and passively aggressive with people, especially those of the opposite sex? Do you rarely express your feelings openly when you're upset, but your behavior signals just how angry you really are? Do you have difficulty prioritizing tasks? Do you procrastinate, finding it difficult to start projects in a timely manner? Or do you have problems ending projects, having multiple projects hanging out there in various stages of completion? Are you in bondage to some form of addiction? Answering yes to any of the above questions will alert you to focus on the time when you were six to twelve years old to discover the roots of these problems.

MARKUS'S STORY (CONTINUED)

Markus grew to manhood, married and had three lovely daughters. Although he was blessed with a lovely family, something was terribly wrong. Markus felt tormented by the fact that his relationship with his daughters, who were 10, 13 and 15 years old, was very unhealthy and destructive. He reported that his relationship with all three daughters always started out wonderfully and remained that way until each of them turned nine years old. Then his relationship with them dramatically changed. Overnight, it became destructive. He found himself being short-tempered, extremely angry, and emotionally and verbally abusive with each one. He constantly reacted to them with the belief that they did not take what he said seriously. He felt as though they did not respect him, his ideas or his feelings. Basically, his relationship with his daughters was in shambles.

Developmental Process

Competition and "The Grass Is Greener"

A new era begins with the advent of school. We now spend long periods of time away from home learning about the world outside the family. We begin developing, testing and fine-tuning skills in many areas. This is the age of healthy competition. Our life is centered on activity, with major emphasis on doing, not feeling. We do things and get into activities because it seems like a good idea at the time, and we don't really consider the consequences of our behavior. Thus, we find the end result of what we sometimes do is less than appreciated by the adults in our life.

"Hey, John! I bet I can throw a rock closer to that window than you can without breaking it!"

"No, you can't!"

Now the competition is on. Rock throwing accuracy is put to the test. We each take turns throwing rocks closer and closer to the window. When all of a sudden, to our chagrin, you miss the mark and the window shatters. Dad comes running out, very upset, angry and quite vocal in his disapproval of your skill-sharpening activity.

"Gee, Dad, why are you so upset? I didn't mean to break the window. We were trying real hard not to break it. What can I say? I missed! I'm a bad shot! All I need is a little more practice!"

It seemed like a good idea at the time. We didn't consider the consequences of our behavior. Parents can use situations like these to instruct in appropriate behavior and teach about the consequences of what we do. Such mishaps do not necessarily indicate that we are a destructive or a delinquent child requiring punishment, but rather that we need parental guidance, instruction and discipline.

It is not only our physical activities that are put to the test; the values, ideals and beliefs of our parents are compared and contrasted with those of our friends' parents. Other adults besides our own parents begin to influence our values and ideals. In this way, we begin learning about the environment outside the family and identifying with society at large. This is necessary so that we can incorporate information about how we fit into society.

When comparisons with other families lead us to conclude that the grass is greener on the other side, we may find that the best solution to this revelation is to run away from home, as one story from my own childhood illustrates.

The day I reported to my father that I was going to run away from home was memorable. What my father did cured me, on the spot, from any future threats to run away. I had reported to dad that I was running away. I was going to live at my friend's house, because I didn't like the rules at home.

Dad said, "Okay." That was it!

I was excited! I ran to my room, packed my bags and turned to leave. There in the doorway, with hands on hips, was my dad.

With an inquisitive voice he asked, "Where are you going with those?" pointing at my bags.

"These are my clothes! I'm running away! I need my clothes!"

He quickly responded, "Drop 'em!" So, I did.

As I stood there in nine-year-old defiance, the competition was on. His next statement shocked me. I tried not to show my surprise.

Dad sternly commanded, "Take off your clothes, all of them!"

Somewhat deflated, but not wanting to show it, I said, "Excuse me?"

Dad repeated loudly, "Take off your clothes!"

More deflated now, I asked, "Why, Dad?"

Then came the statement I will never forget for as long as I live.

Staring deep into my eyes, Dad said, "You came into this world naked; you will go out of this house naked!"

That did it. I repented and asked Dad for permission to stay home and not run away. Dad congratulated me on my excellent decision and then said, "Come down to dinner when you're ready, son."

That worked for me. I never again threatened to run away. I may have thought about it, but I chose to avoid challenging my dad with that again.

Exclusion of the Opposite Sex

Generally, this is the time when social activity and identification are oriented toward the same sex: boys stay with boys, and girls stay with girls. This ensures the discovery and fine-tuning of our sex-role identification. However, some interaction with the opposite sex is also important. This will provide the information we need to be able to relate effectively to the opposite sex in adulthood. Both boys and girls also need involvement with adults of the same sex. In this way we learn appropriate ways of doing things in socio-cultural situations.[2]

It is important during this time that parents continue to provide parental structure, deal with conflicts that arise, encourage the excitement of learning, and set reasonable standards and expectations.

This is an age when we argue and hassle quite a bit. Such behavior is now being used to prove that we are a separate person, an individual. It is a way to test ideas, values and the validity of what we are learning. Mom suffers more from this hassling than dad. This stage of development is to ensure that the earlier stage of mother/child symbiosis remains broken. If it hasn't been broken, as in many cases, these hassles are a further push for the symbiotic break to finally occur. We need to prove to both mom and ourselves that we are a separate person from her—that we are an individual with our own ideas and ways of doing things.

It is important that parents work with their child around this issue of hassling. They need to affirm their child's separateness and teach him/her how to be separate without having to hassle to prove it. Children need to learn that it's okay to think, to have their own ideas and to develop their own ways of doing things. They need to know they can do this and still be cared for and loved by their parents. Hassles and conflicts, then, are normal and necessary. They allow us to define ourselves. Even Father God allows us to argue with Him (see Isa. 43:26). But children do need to learn during times of hassles and arguments how to account for and respect other people's ideas and beliefs. These encounters also encourage them to establish their own reasons for their beliefs and for the things they do, which provide a strong foundation for adult beliefs, values and ideals.

Let's Do Something Else!

There are so many things to do, so much we want to do, that we move from one activity to another. It may appear to parents that we are unable to stay with any one task or activity for any extended period of time, but it is very important now that we are allowed to change activities after a reasonable amount of time without being made to feel like a quitter or like we're being irresponsible. This is the age to learn about a wide range of activities. In this way we learn how to prioritize tasks, how to begin projects and finish them. Such encounters also provide us with the opportunity to assess our skills and talents.

Rather than make their children feel like a quitter and trying to intimidate them into staying with one activity, parents can more appropriately provide them with guidance and direction in starting and stopping activities or tasks.

This is a very industrious stage in life. The child is making foundational decisions about his or her life-plan, vocation and profession. This is the time for dreams and visions that accompany the "When I grow up . . ." statement burning in our hearts. The methods, skills, values and morals we learn and incorporate now provide the material needed to advance into our teen years with excitement, confidence and security. Let's consider some of the more obvious wounds that can occur during these formative years, which result in adult problems.

Weeds and Roots

Let's pick up Markus's story where we left it at the beginning of this chapter.

MARKUS'S STORY (CONTINUED)

During the time of ministry, Markus shared the following: I never saw Mom so full of pain, fear and sadness. I knew she was not only sad and lonely but also worried about having enough money to live. I thought, *I'm now the man of the house. I need to find out how I can make money for Mom and the family.* The majority of my waking hours were occupied with such thoughts. One day Mom sat me down and said, "Markus, you are not to worry about money for this family. You are not responsible for taking care of me financially." How do moms know what sons are thinking? I never said anything about this to her. Mom always seemed to know what was going on with me. It was almost as if she could read my mind. I remember that it was not too long after mom told me not to worry about finances that she made a request of me. One evening, just before bedtime, she asked me to sleep next to her in her bed because she was feeling so lonely, sad and afraid.

I slept in mom's bed that night. I remember feeling very uncomfortable, shameful and angry, but I never spoke a word to mom about my feelings. I didn't want to hurt or upset her any more than she already was. From that night on, I slept with mom until I was 12 years old, when I moved back to my own room. The whole time, I suppressed my feelings of discomfort, shame and anger. I can remember thinking that this was the way I could care for my mom.

Markus was nine years old when his father was killed and he began sleeping in his mother's bed beside her. This stage of development is characterized by a tendency to repress feelings, which is exactly what Markus did. He was unwilling to express his feelings of shame and anger to his mother and so he just covered them up. Yet, this caused a deep wound of resentment in him toward his mother, and he became more argumentative than usual for a child of his age. Passive-aggressive behavior and continuous hassling became characteristic of his relationship with his mom. He could not remember one day when he did not have an argument with her. Subconsciously, he was fighting against the sleeping arrangement, which he found uncomfortable, and was trying to make his statement, more than ever before, that he was separate from her.

As we stated earlier in the chapter, children at this age use hassles and arguments to define their individuality, to prove they are separate, especially from mom. Markus could never resolve his feelings of torment about sleeping with his mom. She wanted him close every night, and he complied. Thus, Markus became stuck in passive-aggressive hassling and argumentative behavior patterns. He was never able to resolve these feelings during the developmental stage when they should have been resolved. Such patterns of behavior continued throughout Markus's life. In fact, these very patterns were characteristic of the relationship he now had with his daughters. He was beginning to discover the roots of this destructive relationship.

Wounds Affect School Performance

The first three years of this developmental stage are crucial for healthy adjustment to formal education provided by public and private school systems. Circumstances can occur during this time that can severely inhibit academic success.

DANIEL'S STORY

Daniel was now 22 years old. When he was seven years old, he had developed an extreme learning disability. He had become dyslexic and was unable to read or comprehend the written word. There were no signs of this problem prior to seven years of age. For 15 years he had struggled with this problem, which was never remediated. Daniel was also tormented by the fear of going crazy, with pervasive feelings of shame, uncleanness and confused sexual identity. He was led by the Holy Spirit to attend the Human Development Seminar, believing that God wanted to heal him and set him free. Thus, he came with high expectations.

During the time of ministry with Daniel, the Lord revealed the sexual abuse he suffered in his family, which he had denied and repressed for years. At about the age of seven, Daniel suffered regular and excessive sexual abuse by his older brother, which went on for several years.

At the time the abuse began, Daniel's ability to function in school was dramatically affected. Overnight, he became unable to read and comprehend. He became overwhelmed with shame and feelings of uncleanness, and was tormented by a belief that he would become mentally insane. This fear of insanity is characteristic of people who have been abused by a family member (incest), as was true in the case of Tamar, Amnon's half-sister, who became desolate after Amnon sexually abused her (see 2 Sam. 13:20). This same potential for desolation exists in all people who are sexually abused by a family member. The one place where children should find safety and protection in this world is in their family. If a child is unable to find safety and protection there, then where else can they possibly find it? Abuse within the family is extremely devastating for children and causes major destruction in their developing young lives.

As we prayed, the Lord revealed Himself to Daniel in a powerfully intense way. He experienced the Lord entering a memory of one of the times when his brother began to abuse him. Jesus suddenly burst into the scene in a blinding light of glory. Spirits of sexual abuse, destruction, perversion and uncleanness that were exposed in the light of the Lord's presence scattered in every direction, fleeing in terror. Daniel, with eyes closed, watched the vision unfold. He reported, "The Lord is dealing with the situation. He's protecting me. He's coming between my brother and me. He's confronting my brother. I feel like the Lord is bringing safety, security and protection into the situation and into my life. Jesus is talking to my brother. I feel like he's commanding every bit of perversion out and away from him." Daniel began praying, taking authority over everything that had tormented him and tried to destroy him for the past 15 years. He knew something had happened.

Late that night, Daniel opened a Bible, and to his amazement he began to read with miraculous fluency. Not only that, but he was also able to understand everything he read. This was a miracle. He shouted with tears of joy, praising the Lord at the top of his voice. He was so excited that he ran throughout the place he was staying, waking people up to show them how he could now read and understand. God had taken away his dyslexia and restored him to wholeness. When the Lord heals, He does a complete work. Daniel, once unable to read and comprehend his native English, has now mastered the Chinese language and is fulfilling his call by ministering in China. All the praise goes to the Lord.

Sharing Daniel's story is not in any way meant to suggest that all learning problems have a root of woundedness that can be traced back to an early stage of development. But Daniel's story and the stories of other individuals recounted in this book clearly show that many people are seriously affected by wounds that occurred at critical points in their development.[3] We believe the Lord wants each of us to be free of the wounds and abuses suffered during childhood in order to fulfill the destiny He has for us.

Injustice: "It's Just Not Fair!"

In this age group the most prevalent area of wounding is in the area of injustice. Many people between the ages of six and twelve years old have been unjustly, even severely punished for behavior that was age appropriate and not meant to cause anyone any harm. They had simply not considered the consequences of their actions.

As we explained earlier, children at this age do things because it seems like a good idea at the time—like the stone-throwing contest earlier in this chapter. Parents need to teach their children the consequences of their behavior and carry out appropriate discipline. However, severe punishment for age-appropriate behavior can and usually does result in wounds that will manifest later in life. Some of the most troubling age-appropriate behaviors that parents are required to deal with at this age are hassling, arguing and fighting. Children use these behaviors to define their individuality and prove that they are separate from mom and dad, sister and brother. So a parent's inappropriate discipline for these behaviors can cause problems later in life.

ROLF'S STORY

Pastor Rolf shared that he lacked true compassion for people. This manifested in hidden feelings of happiness and arrogant sarcasm that rose up from deep inside him when other leaders in opposition to his beliefs had problems in their lives or ministries. Rather than have compassion and pray for them, he would secretly experience satisfaction about their difficulties. He was aware that this attitude was sinful and destructive, and he wanted it out of his life.

As we prayed, the Lord brought Rolf back to the time when he was six to twelve years old. Rolf began to share, "I am three years younger than my brother. We shared the same room during this age, and I remember my brother fighting and hassling with me. My brother was much stronger and always had the advantage in a physical altercation. Our parents would always intervene in our fights and my brother would always get punished, sometimes severely, because my parents said he took advantage of my being so much younger. Even when I provoked the fight, my brother would get punished for it. I remember feeling happy when my brother was punished. Yet, to be honest, the punishment he received was too severe and definitely unjust for most of the situations."

The Lord revealed to Rolf how he had incorporated these feelings and attitudes when he was seven to nine years old, and he had carried them into his adult life so that this way of reacting to the parental punishment suffered by his brother had become a bondage in his life.

As we continued to pray, Rolf remembered one fight for which his brother had received a particularly severe punishment from his parents. The Lord revealed himself in this memory and justly handled the situation between Rolf and his brother. Rolf then took authority over the inappropriate feelings and attitudes that had been strongholds in his life. The Lord also revealed a generational root to the joy and arrogant sarcasm he felt over other people's misfortunes. Rolf's mother and father had modeled this for him and his brother. When people they knew suffered misfortune, they showed no compassion or mercy, but in fact always appeared joyful about it. Rolf prayed and dealt with this stronghold in the generations. He shares that the joy he now feels is not due to people's misfortune but due to the compassion he now feels. He also shares, "The Lord has definitely taken away the arrogant sarcasm and in its place has deposited grace and compassion for others."

Are You a Quitter?

Other problems that result from wounding at this age are procrastination and the tendency to have multiple projects in various stages of completion. These problems may have arisen if your parents didn't understand that this stage of your life was meant as a time for surveying skills and abilities. If out of concern that you would never be able to commit yourself to anything, they forced you to remain at one task or activity, you may now experience difficulties in starting a project and carrying it through to completion, or stopping a project and starting another one. As a result, you may find yourself being one of the many people in this world who have trouble beginning projects. Instead, you work back from deadlines, waiting until the last possible moment to begin and then work furiously to complete the task. Or you may have no problem beginning projects—in fact, you easily begin them and have a number in progress—but you have difficulty in bringing them to completion.

The people we have ministered to with such problems have found healing by focusing on the damage they have suffered as a result of parental pressure to stick to one activity during this time of their life. It would be appropriate to add here that we are not proposing that children of this age should not be taught to persevere in some things. Yet, when a parent always evaluates his child's desire to begin something new as an inability to persevere, it can cause the types of problems we've mentioned if handled inappropriately.

Is God able to do the things we share in these chapters? Yes! He is not only able, but also He is definitely willing. Our responsibility is to admit that we are in bondage and to desire to be free. It is God's responsibility to do it.

Addiction: The Essence of Destruction

The last problem to consider here is that of addiction. Our intention here is not in any way to refute the many long-standing and comprehensive studies on the causes of addiction, nor to attempt to give our own all-inclusive theory. However, in our ministry to numerous people who were in bondage to some form of addiction, we have observed a functional-developmental component to the problem that we hope, when added to the other research, will increase understanding about this very destructive problem.

As we have previously explained, the six- to twelve-year-old stage of development is a time of industry, of engaging in many activities in order to discover, develop and fine-tune the skills, talents and abilities children will carry into adulthood. These are skills that will ensure success in a profession, in the family, in the community and in society at large. However, in certain situations, a person will almost inevitably become susceptible to the bondage of addiction.

People may become prey to an addiction as a result of being made to feel inadequate, inferior and/or helpless in their abilities, skills and talents during this stage of development. This happens as a result of not being allowed or encouraged to develop their own ways of doing things. Instead, mom stepped in and did many of the things for them that they should have been learning to do on their own. It may have been wonderful. Mom may even have felt that she wanted to do these tasks for them because she loved them so much. Or maybe she was doing more for them than necessary because she was trying to compensate for the lack of a father in their life. Whatever the reasons, this was destructive to their developing a sense of adequacy in life. They were made to remain dependent on their mother when they should have been learning to solve their own problems and learning ways of doing things for themselves. They were being trained to be dependent. They were not being trained to develop their own capabilities and adequacies to succeed in life as an adult.

Adolescence, then, became an extremely stormy time for such people because they were having to cope with these deficiencies. As a result, they experienced feelings of such inferiority and inadequacy that they needed something to depend on in order to make it in the world. Having not been taught to develop their own thinking and doing, they were not equipped to meet the challenges of adolescence with a foundation of self-developed skills and talents already in place. They began feeling inferior, inadequate, helpless and unable to think independently. They may not even have felt in the least bit confident in their ability to solve problems or deal with difficult situations. Of course they didn't admit to any of this. They were grown up now. They were too "with it" to admit to such weakness. Now, pride entered to influence and assist them in the end result which, we believe, is the ultimate goal of all addictions: to bring destruction.

One additional ingredient must be considered. Since feelings are repressed at this stage of development more than at any other, these six- to twelve-year-olds may not be prepared for the resurgence of intense emotions at the onslaught of adolescence. They may have no way of dealing with these overwhelming feelings, especially if their parents have not provided an environment within which feelings can be expressed and dealt with; and so they have to find some other way of handling the problem. Having been trained in dependency up until now, they will continue in what they have learned. They will find something (or someone) outside of themselves on which to become dependent. They will turn to anything that can keep their feelings under control—anything they can depend on to help them through the stormy challenges they are now facing in their life.

It is important to note that they will choose something (or someone) that will assist them in what they believe about themselves: something that concurs with their view that they are inadequate, inferior and helpless to do anything effective on their own; that they are unable to think, solve problems and deal effectively with the difficult situations in life. If father, mother or family members in past generations have had problems with addictions, then they are quite likely to follow the same destructive pattern. Addictions provide a false sense of comfort. They mask feelings of inadequacy, inferiority and helplessness. They continue the life pattern of being dependent on something or someone outside of themselves. Ultimately, they bring to completion the deep-seated belief that a person's only way out is to destroy him or herself.

It is quite probable that some people who are reading this are themselves struggling with some form of addiction. Please hear God's heart. He is much bigger than any addiction you are struggling with. He is more powerful than any bondage. As we minister to those under the oppression of addiction, the Lord faithfully reveals Himself as the Supreme Authority. He destroys every bondage and stronghold that addictions have over His people. He drives out the spiritual forces that accompany all addictions. He then moves to heal the multiple wounds inflicted by the cloak of dependency thrown over you. He puts to death inadequacy, inferiority and helplessness. In their place He builds up, encourages and edifies.

This is His new beginning for you. Then it is time for you to do your part. Specific behavior patterns are characteristic of all addictions, and you will need to change them in order to work out what Jesus works in. You will need to commit to major changes in these old behaviors. Each day, you will need to receive direction from the Lord in what, when and how to do things. Obviously, this requires you to draw close to Jesus, to depend upon Him for everything. But isn't that what we all need to do?

Father God's Intervention

BACK TO MARKUS

The Lord revealed to Markus the overwhelming effect the unspoken feelings he experienced at nine years old had had on his life since that time. And because Markus had been unable to speak to his mom about his feelings, he was now displacing these old feelings of resentment and anger on his daughters. The Lord also gave Markus the understanding that his relationship with his daughters became destructive when they turned nine years old. This was the same age Markus was when the problem started for him with his mother. His daughters' turning nine years old was the catalyst that ignited all the nine-year-old feelings he carried for his mom. What a revelation this was for Markus!

The Lord then began to reveal Himself to Markus in a memory he had of being in his mother's bed. He reported, "The Lord is removing me from Mom's bed. He's revealing to me that the care of Mom's emotions and her life are His responsibility, not mine." Markus then released his mom to the Lord, renouncing all the shame, resentment and anger he had toward his mom, and letting it go. The Lord healed the wounds in Markus and began to input into his life the appropriate fathering he needed so that he could care for his daughters in a healthy, loving way.

Markus knew the next step in this process was to deal with each daughter individually. He needed to share what the Lord had revealed to him and healed him of. He made a commitment to ask his daughters to forgive him and to pray with each daughter and ask the Lord to heal them of every wound he had caused in their young lives.

The Lord Jesus has done all that is necessary for our healing: He endured the cross (see Heb. 12:2) and despised the shame; He took all our infirmities, sickness and disease (see Isa. 53:5). It is our responsibility to recognize areas of bondage in our lives; to desire freedom from them; to ask the Lord to set us free; to receive what the Lord deposits in each of these areas; to do what He instructs us to do. It is a simple procedure yet so difficult for those of us who are plagued by the most ancient hindrance to God's work in our lives: *pride*. But this can also be torn down and trampled under our feet by humbling ourselves before the Lord.

CHRISTIAN'S STORY

Christian remembered clearly the day he rounded the corner on his way home from a friend's house where he had spent the night. As he turned the corner, he saw his house engulfed in flames. In a surreal nightmare of reality, the shock distanced him from the screaming sirens of fire engines rushing past him to the scene. He stood frozen in disbelief for what seemed like hours as neighbors ran past him. Finally, he moved hesitantly toward the house, fearing the worst. Christian vaguely recalls a neighbor coming to console him. Both his parents were killed in the fire. All he could think in that moment was, "What am I going to do?" He was only nine years old.

As an adult, Christian, now an expert consultant on Personal Safety for the Home and Workplace, needed to be healed and restored from the devastation of sudden abandonment that left him an orphan. In the healing experience, the Lord spoke to

Christian and told him that his chosen profession was also part of God's plan to redeem. Although he was not able to prevent his parents' death, he had been used by God to prevent the harm and death of others as he taught Personal Safety. The Lord had redeemed the tragedy of Christian's life and was working it out for good.

We have seen this many times over the years: police officers raised in family violence now working to protect; gifted entrepreneurs raised in poverty now financing opportunities for orphans and others bound in poverty; physicians who grew up with the devastation of sickness and disease in their families now bringing healing. Often God redeems in this way as well—turning what the enemy meant for harm to great good.

Truth: Facing the Pain

The pain of injustice is not always easy to recognize in itself, but it becomes clear in our behavior. This wounding makes us vulnerable to offense whenever we encounter injustice. We can be so sensitized to injustice that we are too easily offended and can be predisposed to carrying the offenses of others. With this perspective, it is easy for us to fall into the false belief that we are to dash about on our white horses "righting all wrongs." It seems like a noble pursuit, but in the end it only leads to exhaustion and, at its worst, can bind us up in offenses we have no power to resolve because they are not ours. It is time to face the truth:

There is a way that seems right to a man, but in the end it leads to death (Prov. 14:12).

Revelation: Revisiting the Scene

Ask the Holy Spirit to reveal what happened in your life between six and twelve years of age. Injustice and other problems rooted in this time of life directly hinder the release of your gifts and callings. Sometimes even being able to recognize the gifts and callings in your life depends on what you experienced in this time of development. Jesus will never leave you. He will be there with you to walk through whatever you need to face from your childhood. It's time to get free.

Redemption: Healing and Deliverance

The Lord wants to release you from the pain of injustice and insecurity regarding your abilities. He wants to listen to your thoughts and feelings and help you sort out the internal conflicts you struggle with. He will be your advocate and establish justice in those unjust situations you were wounded by. Most of all, He wants to revive your gifts and callings and encourage you to dream again.

> A bruised reed he will not break, and a smoldering wick he will not snuff out. In faithfulness he will bring forth justice; he will not falter or be discouraged till he establishes justice on earth (Isa. 42:3-4).

Restoration: The Planting of the Lord

You were born for a purpose, and the Lord wants to restore your eternal destiny. Whatever has happened to destroy the dream in your heart, the Lord will plant it again and nurture it to maturity as you listen to Him, believe His Word and obey what He asks you to do. It is not too late! All things are possible in Him.

Reparenting: Father God, "Father" Me

Probably the greatest challenge for all of us at this stage of development was learning how to argue our point of view in a healthy, respectful way. It is impossible to learn how to do this without practice and correction. We need to get into the struggle with Father God and work through it with Him. He even invites us to do it: "Review the past for me, let us argue the matter together" (Isa. 43:26).

God always wins, but He is willing to hear us out, and that is the "fathering" we most needed then, and the "fathering" we most need now.

THE FATHER'S HEALING PROCESS:
STEPS TO HEALING, FREEDOM AND RESTORATION

Healing

1. Identify the adult problems—behaviors or attitudes that apply to you. (See Tables 6A/6B: Healthy/Unhealthy Development.)

2. Ask the Holy Spirit to reveal the root cause of each problem. The root is whatever happened to you between six and twelve years of age that caused a wounding in your life and allowed the problem to take root. This revelation may be in the form of a memory, a picture, an impression, a thought, an awareness or some other way of "knowing" (see Luke 8:17).

3. Ask Jesus to reveal His Presence there with you. The presence of the Lord changes things (see Ps. 31:14-16; Heb. 13:5-6,8).

4. Tell Jesus what you are feeling and thinking in this revealed time, place, experience. Listen to His response (see Pss. 88:1; 91:14-16).

5. Ask Jesus to reveal what the Father intended for this time of your life. Jesus comes to show us the Father. Allow the Lord to minister to you; rest in Him and take time to receive what you need. He comes to care for your developmental needs, to heal you, to redeem all that was lost to you and to restore you to be all He created you to be (see Jer. 29:11; Matt. 15:13).

Freedom

6. In the name of Jesus, break the power of the lie that was planted in your heart from the wound, and ask the Lord to uproot it. Embrace the truth—the Word of God—that has the power to set you free. Proclaim the promises in God's Word that are His answers to your need (see Matt. 15:13; John 8:31-32; 2 Cor. 1:20).

7. Identify any pattern of sin, bondage or curses passed from generation to generation in your family. Break any generational curses, if necessary (see also Appendix A: Generational Curses). Forgive your parents and all those who wounded you (see Matt. 6:14; Gal. 3:13-14).

8. Take authority, in Jesus' name, over any demonic oppression or influences in your life that the Lord has revealed. In the name of Jesus and His authority, command them to leave (see Luke 10:19; Jas. 4:7).

Restoration

9. Receive Father God as your eternal Father and receive your inheritance of life in Christ Jesus. Seek the Father each day to father you (see John 10:10; Heb. 12:10).

10. Ask the Holy Spirit to teach you how to walk in your "newness of life." Commit to listen to and obey the Holy Spirit and begin to put God's Word into action in your life (see John 14:26; 16:13; Phil. 2:12-13).

Table 6A: Healthy Development

Stage of Life	Significant Issues	Developmental Task (needed for healthy development)	Adult Manifestation
6 Years to 12 Years	Skill development/gifts and callings Argue, hassle, disagree Competition Skill learning	Establish separate identity Find own methods of doing things Life skills surveyed and developed Learn how to learn Task priority and completion Values and rules connected to reasons	Prioritize activities Complete tasks Creative in problem solving Healthy development of social and emotional skills Strong sense of values and rules, applied with grace Confident in own methods of doing things Secure in challenges of life Knowing and fulfilling God's plan in life

Table 6B: Unhealthy Development

Stage of Life	Significant Issues	Developmental Task (needed for healthy development)	Adult Manifestation
6 Years to 12 Years	Skill development	Rules and values too rigid	Inflexible with rules and values
	Argue, hassle, disagree	Rules or values lacking or inconsistent	Problems with task priority and task completion
	Competition	Unable to argue rules with reasons	Addictive personality traits
	Skill learning	Made to stick to one task or activity	Passive-aggressive behavior
		How to start and stop projects not taught	Compelled to war against injustice
		Punishment harsh and unjust	Use feelings on others to control
			Use feelings on self to punish; guilt-ridden
			Unaware of God's plan for life
			Insecure in gifts and callings

7

INTEGRATING, CONNECTING, MATURING

The Early Teen Years

GRAHAM'S STORY

Since the time of his teen years, Graham had been overwhelmed by severe insecurities and panic, especially when speaking publicly or in a business context. He was literally paralyzed by fear and insecurity. He also struggled with symbiotic relationships, being far too dependent on others for his own sense of worth. He could not understand why he was experiencing these problems. What had happened in his teen years? What had changed?

The teen years: Instilled deep in our psyche are the lifelong impressions of the agony and ecstasy of those tumultuous years. Emotional reawakening and surging hormones herald the onset of adolescence when we shake off the long emotional dormancy of the previous years (which focused on *doing* rather than *feeling*) and we begin to feel again. The focus now is on social skillfulness, with friends and relationships a high priority. Tasks, studies and the like tend to fall like a brick to the bottom of our conscious awareness.

God in His wisdom built redemption into the developmental process during the teen years. Adolescence is the bridge between childhood and adult life, providing an opportunity for us to revisit all the earlier stages of development for a final resolution of issues.[1] It is a chance to correct and complete unfinished business from the earlier developmental stages. Since it is also the time when our sexual identity begins to mature, puberty adds an interesting twist to the adolescent process.

Adolescent resolution involves the integrating of earlier development with the relationship skills and life skills being developed in the teen years. If integration is successful, the complete, mature person will function effectively as an individual and will have the capability to initiate and maintain healthy relationships. However, successful integration is rare. The wounds of our early life hinder our maturing process and there is a sense of déjà vu as we confront certain problems over and over again. We find ourselves going around the mountain only to find ourselves back in the same spot time after time, seemingly unable to get out of the rut and move on. The apostle Paul said it best:

> I do not understand what I do. For what I want to do I do not do, but what I hate I do. . . . For what I do is not the good I want to do; no, the evil I do not want to do—this I keep on doing. . . . What a wretched man I am! Who will rescue me from this body of death? Thanks be to God— through Jesus Christ our Lord! (Rom. 7:15,19,24-25).

What is happening?

Adult Problems

Trouble in early teen years shows up in adult life in a variety of ways. Specific adult problems rooted in this stage of development are:

- difficulty with time structuring and task priority
- struggle with thinking and problem solving
- insecurity regarding limits
- symbiotic relationships
- inappropriate expression of anger
- eating disorders
- addictions

GRAHAM'S STORY (CONTINUED)

Graham's mother had died when he was 10 years old, and his father remarried when he was about 13 years old. His stepmother proved to be the antithesis of his own natural mother. All the good that she had woven into his life was systematically undone under the severe emotional abuse of his stepmother. She railed at him from dawn 'til dusk; nothing he did was good enough for her. Her tirades and curses terrorized Graham, leaving him with bouts of fear and insecurity to deal with, even into his adult life, which often undermined his personal and professional success.

To understand better how these problems get a foothold, it is important to consider what is needed for healthy development in the early teen years.

Developmental Process

Oral issues, time structuring, anger, rebellion, opposition and independence are all challenges teens face. If you have been around young teens, you are probably aware of the "mouth" issues. "In the head and out the mouth," as the old saying goes. The fine art of discretion has not yet been mastered. Generally speaking, girls are into the "snap, crackle, popping" of chewing gum and talking nonstop to relieve oral stress, while boys are exploring the range and variety of noises that the human mouth is capable of—you will often hear them coming long before you see them. Eating everything in sight is a favorite pastime for boys at this age. Of course, there are exceptions to every rule, and both boys and girls can indulge in these annoying habits. This oral agitation is one signal that early adolescence has arrived.

In our early teens, we are not self-starters when it comes to anything vaguely related to task or work. Parental guidance is essential now to learn task priority and time structuring. Even the most diligent, task-oriented individuals hit a bit of a slump in this early transition. The good news is that it's normal. This is not to say we should be allowed to be irresponsible, but it helps to know it is normal. We are learning how to balance responsibilities with social relationships.

Also normal now are bouts of anger, rebellion and opposition as we struggle to establish our individuation.

Developmental Needs: Twelve to Thirteen Years Old

The earliest stages of development are now being recycled. Young teens often seem to regress in their maturity, causing parents great consternation; but understanding "recycling" can help put things into perspective. Issues from babyhood are resurfacing to be resolved. Young teens often exhibit behavior reminiscent of "baby days"—they love to eat, sleep, play and cry. They become nostalgic about the "good old days" of symbiosis, when mom did all the "work stuff." Young teens want mom to take care of them and do things for them again. In short, young teens try to reestablish symbiosis. The parents' task now is to resist dependency. Teens need to learn how to ask for what they need and learn that asking is the way to get taken care of. The Scriptures confirm this truth: "Ask and it will be given to you. . . . For everyone who asks receives" (Matt. 7:7-8). Jesus said it!

Teen Brain Study

Jay Giedd, neuroscientist at the National Institute of Mental Health, has researched the teen brain and made some revolutionary discoveries. Using MRI technology, he has documented an amazing growth spurt in the brain that was unknown before. "In the frontal part of the brain, the part of the brain involved in judgment, organization, planning, strategizing—those very skills that teens get better and better at—this process of thickening of the gray matter peaks at about age 11 in girls and age 12 in boys, roughly about the same time as puberty."[2] Since this part of the brain is essentially under construction, it accounts for some of the unusual behaviors in teens that we often blamed on hormones or rebellion. It provides a new source to understand teen behavior and be able to provide the support and guidance needed.

In our young teen years, we are very self-critical and insecure. We need affection and affirmation, as well as correction. Painfully aware of our every flaw and failure, we need some honest encouragement and genuine praise to help us weather the intensity of self-criticism we inflict on ourselves.[3]

Time Structuring

Teens need to learn time structuring. They are not self-starters at this stage: When it comes to tasks, they need structure. It is important for them to learn to order time so that they are able to get everything done that they are responsible for. It is also imperative for them to have input to help them establish reasonable time frames for completing their studies, chores, and so on. Teens need to experience this mutual respect and cooperation with parents in order to learn healthy submission to authority.

Sexuality

Puberty gives rise to a natural curiosity about sexuality. Teens need clear, accurate information from a healthy, godly perspective. Without this, they are vulnerable to searching out information on their own from various sources, not all of which will provide them with healthy options.

Boundaries and Limits

With the reawakening of feelings, young teens now crave sensory stimulation. Structure and boundaries are needed for protection as they begin to explore again. Curiosity and the lure of sensory stimulation can lead to experimentation with substances such as drugs and alcohol. This can be a very destructive period if there is too much freedom. Young teens need as much supervision as they did when they were toddlers, with boundaries and limits clearly defined. Boundaries and limits are not there to restrict young people, but to protect them. They have a false perception that they can handle their own lives and do not need to be treated "like a baby." In fact, they need to be protected and watched over in their ever-expanding exploration of the world.

Real Values

Teens at this stage begin to identify with "real values." They test family values to decide which values they will incorporate and live their lives by. When they see adults living according to the values they profess, they are much more likely to accept and incorporate those values into their own life.

Developmental Needs: Fourteen Years Old

Anger, opposition and rebellion are the hallmarks of this age. The fight is on for separation and independence. Individuation is the goal. Testing authority and negativity are on the rise again. This is the sequel to the two-year-old phase, revisited in a bigger body! "NO" is the teen's war cry of independence! Often they oppose adults just to assert their separation from them. No matter what adults say, some teens will be oppositional just to be different. On the other side there is a strong tendency to conform to peers to be accepted. Anger erupts and they are engulfed in negativity. The pressure is on—they must think and solve problems and meet social demands and responsibilities, all while their hormones are raging. Often growth spurts cause them to feel awkward in their own bodies and they can sometimes be a bit testy. In the early teen years, they are masters of reverse psychology: They hassle parents to give in to their demands, but deep down they really don't want them to. Truth is, they want and respect strong parents who model what they require of their teens and are willing to be the "bad guys" and set unpopular limits when necessary.

Anger

Inappropriate expression of anger signals a need for parenting. Overstepping boundaries is a way of testing authority. *Do you really mean what you say?* Teens will attempt to shift responsibility at this age: it's the "make me do something" stage. At 14, teens need to learn how to manage their anger appropriately. As Scripture says, "In your anger do not sin" (Eph. 4:26). Anger is an ever-present reality to teens at this stage, which makes it a prime time to learn and incorporate the healthy management of anger.

Many Christians struggle with what to do with anger, most often because of misguided beliefs that are not scriptural. Anger is not sin. What we do with it can be if we don't learn to manage it for good. God's anger is recorded several times in the Old Testament (for example, Ps. 18:7-15), and Jesus rearranged the furniture in the temple outer courts in righteous anger (see John 2:13-17). Neither the Father nor Jesus ever sinned, so it must be possible to be angry and not sin. Anger is an emotion given by God that energizes us to action in order to deal with problems and correct wrongs.

The following practical steps are very helpful in beginning to learn anger management:

1. Years of built-up anger and resentment need to be released to the Lord. It is too overwhelming to process all that backlog on our own. If there are any specific circumstances that need to be dealt with, the Lord will reveal them and direct you through the process (see Heb. 12:15).

2. Recognize your anger. Acknowledge it when you feel it (see Eph. 4:26).

3. Anger has energy: externalize the energy of the anger. Verbally expelling it may be enough for small frustrations, like being left alone to clean up after a church fellowship gathering. But greater anger may require more physical activity to release it. For such occasions, cleaning the house, garage, tearing up overgrown gardens can be effective; or for the sports-minded, running, cycling, soccer and the like can offer the needed release. This helps to focus the energy of the anger in a constructive way.

4. Go to the Lord and sort it out with Him first. He will help you get your heart right (see Ps. 139:23-24).

5. Go to the one who has wronged you and work out the offense (see Matt. 18:15-17).

6. Pursue resolution and reconciliation (see 2 Cor. 5:18-19).

7. Pursue peace. Develop a practical strategy to avoid the same problem in the future (see Ps. 34:14; 1 Pet. 3:11).

Thinking

At this stage it is important to integrate thinking and problem solving more fully. Taking personal responsibility for behavior, being held accountable and facing the natural consequences for their choices are all important for character development. Breaking symbiosis with mom, once and for all, is essential in order to become a fully functioning, responsible individual.

Social Contract

If all has gone well, teens emerge from this time with a clear social contract. The social contract, in essence, is, "There are things I must do in life, whether I want to or not, whether I feel like it or not. Other people have feelings about what I do, and I must consider others. The world does not revolve around me." Needless to say, there are many people in the world who have not gotten this insight yet.

Decisions About Life and Self

The experiences teens have during this time of development result in an impression about themselves that becomes part of their belief system. They may come to the conclusion that there is or there is not an order to their life; they can or they cannot think and solve their own problems; they are or they are not separate from their parents, especially mom. Ultimately, what they believe to be true about themselves will affect their thinking and behavior. "As [a man] thinks in his heart, so is he" (Prov. 23:7, NKJV) is a powerful truth.

Weeds and Roots

The problems that take root at this time of life have a direct impact on our adult years. The wounds of the first months of life will also come up for resolution during the early teen years, as the following story poignantly illustrates.

THE STORY OF A CONTENTIOUS SON

A mother came for counseling regarding her 13-year-old son. He had always been resistant to her from the time he was a baby, but now the contentiousness was becoming increasingly more hostile. As we prayed and asked the Lord to show us the root of this problem, He took her back to the early months of the boy's life. The mother had been ambivalent about having another child, since her husband was often traveling away from home and she had to care for the children on her own most of the time. Her husband, however, had wanted another child and had promised her he would be home more to help care for the family. She relented and soon become pregnant.

In the first months of her pregnancy, he had been more attentive and present to care for the family, but just before the son was to be born, the father had fallen back into old habit patterns, and she had felt betrayed and abandoned. Deep resentment for her husband and bitterness had grown in her heart. As the mother nursed her son in bitterness and resentment, he became deeply wounded. When he rejected the breast, his mother was forced to bottle-feed him. As he grew more independent, he pulled away from his mother and grew increasingly resistant, even rejecting, in his reactions to her. He would not allow her to be close to him. Over the years, the mother felt "a wall" between them.

In the prayer time, the Lord revealed that her son had sensed the resentment she had felt for her husband. But her son had the impression it was against him and so, in defense, he had pulled away from her to survive. She was shocked, totally unaware of the impact her heart attitudes had had on her son. As she prayed and repented before the Lord, we asked the Lord to heal his wounds and restore them to right relationship.

A few hours later, she called to tell us of the miraculous change in her son. She had gone to pick him up from soccer practice. During the drive home, he began to share how he had realized how mean he had been to her and asked his mom to forgive him. He didn't know why he had been like that. She was able to share with him what the Lord had revealed in the time of ministry and asked him to forgive her. They then prayed together for the Lord to heal and restore them and their relationship. As they hugged for the first time in years, she knew the Lord had done a miracle of restoration.

Pain and Addictions

With the onset of the teen years comes the reawakening of feelings. For those who have had a relatively stable, healthy childhood, this is merely a new phase of their development as a person. But for others, the reawakening of feelings brings the resurgence of deep pain and shame, which has remained unresolved from the early years. Dealing with these feelings can be excruciating and bewildering, particularly when added to the stresses they are already facing. The disabling pain and shame often drive young teens to drugs and alcohol to "medicate" the symptoms. The root of drug and alcohol addiction is pain. It is critical to get to the pain to get free, but this is not an easy task after years of repressed feelings. It is easy to move into denial and keep the pain buried in order to avoid having to face it. The problem is exacerbated when the teen develops a tolerance level to the drug or alcohol and it takes increasingly larger amounts to get the relief he or she craves. With the help of the Holy Spirit, and the focus on the pain, it is possible to get to the root cause and experience the healing necessary to quell the need for addiction.

Eating Disorders

In the United States of America, about 7 million women and 1 million men are afflicted with an eating disorder. One in 10 cases of anorexia nervosa leads to death from starvation, cardiac arrest or suicide, according to the National Institute for Mental Health.[4] Girls traditionally have been more susceptible to eating disorders; however this is currently changing as boys are feeling similar pressures to be thin and muscular. "Ten to 24 percent of male adolescents report bingeing, and 1 to 2 percent report engaging in vomiting or use of laxatives or diuretics."[5] Male athletes pushed to maintain low weight are especially susceptible to the development of eating disorders. "A study of 84 German university athletes (wrestlers and rowers) reported that 52 percent engaged in binge eating and 11 percent had a number of eating disorder symptoms."[6]

Eating disorders often surface in the teen years. The most common are anorexia nervosa, bulimia nervosa and compulsive eating. Clinical treatment often involves a team approach, as the disorders touch on many areas of a person's life. These disorders have a complex root system involving addiction, generational curses, wounding in the feeding process, controlling environments, sexual abuse and other trauma or emotional pain. Getting healed of the wounds that started the problem, and being set free from the bondages associated with it, is only the beginning for the person with an eating disorder. The most effective course of action is a combination of prayer ministry and counseling, providing practical information, support and accountability. Let's take a brief look at each in turn.

Anorexia Nervosa

Anorexia nervosa is characterized by self-starvation and excessive weight loss. The individual experiences an intense fear of gaining weight, a feeling of being fat even though underweight and a denial of the seriousness of the low body weight. Physical problems that are associated with this disorder include damage to the heart and other vital organs, low blood pressure, slow heartbeat, abdominal pain, loss of muscle mass, constipation and sensitivity to cold.[7]

Bulimia Nervosa

Bulimia nervosa is characterized by a secretive cycle of binge eating followed by purging through vomiting, using laxatives and diuretics or compulsive exercise in order to prevent weight gain. The person feels a lack of control over eating behaviors during binges and has a preoccupation with weight, body shape and appearance.

Complications associated with bulimia include damage to the heart, kidneys, reproductive system, intestinal track, esophagus, teeth and mouth.[8]

Compulsive Eating/Binge Eating

Binge eating disorder is a syndrome in which an individual eats large amounts of food in a short period of time and feels a lack of control over eating during the binge. The person consumes food more rapidly than normal, eats until uncomfortably full, ingests large amounts although not physically hungry and eats alone due to a sense of embarrassment. Feelings of distress and intense feelings of depression or guilt follow.

The sufferer may undertake sporadic fasts or repetitive diets, and therefore body weight may fluctuate from normal to obese. Physical complications associated with this disorder include diabetes, hypertension, circulatory problems, degenerative joint disease, hormonal imbalances and cardiovascular disease.[9]

ANIKA'S STORY

Anika was alarmingly frail when we first met her. Gaunt and ashen, she gazed at us through lifeless, hollowed eyes. There was an urgency in the Spirit to get to the root cause of this horrifying oppression in her life. She was bound in denial and deception and had no understanding of what was happening to her or why. Before we could even move into healing prayer, we needed to take authority over the spiritual forces of deception and denial, in Jesus' name (see Luke 10:19), and command the "god of this world blinding her mind" to remove the blinders so that she could see the truth (see 2 Cor. 4:4). When we asked the Lord to reveal the root, He gave us a picture of Anika's mother nursing her as an infant. She was obsessive about her baby's weight and would not feed her very much. As a result of never being allowed to take in sufficient nourishment, Anika was always on the edge of hunger. Since her mom was pleased that Anika was tiny, Anika incorporated the association, "Mom is pleased when I am starving." The Lord also revealed that addiction was in the family and Anika had inherited that bondage as well. Anika asked the Lord to reveal Himself in her memory. He took Anika in His arms and gave her a bottle, which she devoured and another besides, as He encouraged her to take in nourishment until she was satisfied. In that experience the Lord uprooted the lie that she must starve to please her mother. He exposed the deception that blinded her from seeing how her body really looked, and he restored a healthy appetite. Anika prayed to break the generational bondage of addiction and broke agreement with the spirit of death, in Jesus' name, embracing the gift of life He gave her. He released her from the hold of the enemy and set her free to live. After this session, she continued in counseling, knowing she needed to learn how to work out her healing. She needed to learn how to eat in a healthy way and how to have a healthy perception of her body. Today she is a healthy young woman with a strong athletic build, as God created her to be.

HANNAH'S STORY

Hannah was a beautiful young woman, but she was seriously overweight, which was the reason she came for ministry and counseling. She wanted to get her fluctuating weight under control. She would have extreme weight fluctuations from the obese condition she was currently in to near starvation after prolonged fasting. She felt trapped in this pendulum of destruction, never having been able to break the cycle. When we asked the Holy Spirit to reveal the root cause of this perplexing cycle, He revealed Hannah in the womb. Hannah saw herself as a tiny, tiny baby. When we asked the Lord what this meant, He showed us Hannah's mom, who was only a young teen, weeping and fearful. As we prayed, the Lord revealed that Hannah's mom had conceived Hannah out of wedlock and, fearing her father's wrath, was trying to hide the pregnancy. She was not eating, thinking this would keep her from gaining weight and being discovered. What she did not realize in her youth was that she was seriously jeopardizing her baby's health. By the time the pregnancy was discovered and she was taken to the doctor, the baby was in crisis. The doctor rebuked the young woman and told her if she did not eat, her baby would die. Not ever having intended to hurt the baby, Hannah's mom went into alarm and started overeating to compensate. Hannah survived, but in her subconscious was indelibly imprinted a compulsive eating pattern that triggered in her adolescence and continued into her adult life. She fasted until she nearly starved, then compulsively overate to the point of gorging, until she was dangerously obese. Although she had been in counseling for years, she had not been able to break free from the compulsion. In the prayer time, the Lord broke the curse and the destructive cycle, and she broke the power of the addictive spiritual forces driving her. The freedom from bondages and patterns imposed on her in the womb made it possible for her to incorporate the healthy eating habits she had been learning.

Individuals troubled by eating disorders need to be released from generational bondages and spiritual forces of addiction and compulsion (see Appendix A), and they need healing prayer for wounds and wrong associations in the feeding process, and for freedom from control and oppression in family relationships. They are then able to begin to make healthy choices that are right for them. Counseling is most effective after a person is set free in the Spirit and has walked through a healing experience with the Lord to see when the problem took root.

Hypocrisy

Teens are very sensitive in this time of development to inconsistencies in the lives of authority figures and can be deeply wounded by hypocrisy. Hypocrisy fuels the fires of rebellion and erodes respect for authority. Without healthy, godly role models, they are set adrift and have a hard time identifying and incorporating values by which to live their lives. It is especially destructive when someone they looked up to and admired in Christian leadership fails them. The sense of betrayal and mistrust can be overwhelming and difficult to come to terms with at this tender age, and its effects can carry over into adult life, causing skepticism and cynicism, and making it hard for them to submit to rightful authority.

Insecurity

Insecurity is also rooted in this time of development. Insecurity regarding limits, ego boundaries and expectations all come as a result of insufficient parenting. One of the biggest mistakes parents make now is to assume that young teens are as mature on the inside as they appear to be on the outside and give them too much freedom without enough adult supervision. Insufficient limits and boundaries can leave young people vulnerable in a world of challenges and confrontations they are not yet emotionally prepared to deal with. Too much freedom too soon can be very destructive, causing serious wounding and long-term negative repercussions into adult life. For young teens to feel secure, they must be given clear limits and boundaries. They need as much protection now as they did when they were toddlers; without it, they get hurt.

Symbiosis and Dependency Reinforced

Equally harmful now is reinforcing dependency by allowing the symbiosis to be reestablished. If this happens, people remain helpless and dependent, and spend their whole life seeking out symbiotic relationships. Too often moms are not willing to allow their sons to grow up and they keep them dependent by doing everything for them. Because most boys do not want to hurt mom, they stay dependent and get stuck in immaturity, which gives rise to all kinds of problems in adult life, especially in relationships. Individuals who have never broken symbiosis wander through life with an invisible umbilical cord, on a mission to seek out and connect up with people who will take care of them and satisfy their unmet needs. This is "mission impossible" unless they connect with Jesus. Only He can fill their emptiness and be the strength in their weakness.

Displaced Anger

Learning to manage anger in a healthy way is one of teens' most important needs at this stage. Displaced anger or inappropriate expression of anger leads to sin and often results in someone getting hurt. This usually happens because parents do not know how to deal appropriately with their own anger—another case of you cannot give what you do not have.

The sin of anger can have the following consequences:

1. It can hurt others physically or emotionally.
2. It can destroy property.
3. It can hurt self.

Most of us would agree immediately that the first two are sin, but the third one is the sin we commit most often. We hurt ourselves by holding anger inside instead of feeling it and learning to express it appropriately to bring needed change.

Internalizing anger is self-destructive in the following ways:

1. People may swallow their anger because they were not given permission to be angry in their family as they were growing up, or they saw too much violent anger and vowed never to be angry themselves. Usually, they end up unloading the anger inappropriately by displacing it onto someone. The resulting feelings of shame lead to a renewed vow not to be angry and, thus, the cycle starts again. This is very destructive in relationships.

2. Denying and repressing anger lead to depression, hypertension, colitis, ulcers and a myriad of other stress disorders. In the extreme, unresolved resentment has been linked to rheumatoid arthritis.

3. Unrestrained, nurtured anger also results in serious physical disorders and is especially harmful to the cardiac system.

Sexuality

At this age, teens are naturally curious about sex and need to be given accurate information. Lack of information or insufficient information compels them to seek out other sources. Often they consult their friends, which can be the blind leading the blind, so to speak, and we know how that ends up. Even worse, they may end up turning to pornographic material and media or other questionable resources to satisfy the need to know. This covert searching opens the door to perversion and can lead to addiction.

Father God's Intervention
GRAHAM'S STORY (CONTINUED)

Graham hesitated—even the thought of facing that painful time again seemed unbearable. Yet, living in fear and torment was an even more painful option. As we prayed and asked the Lord to reveal the root of Graham's problems, he saw the situation in a new light. Not only was he oppressed by his stepmother, but his father was also under her control. Graham had needed his father to protect him, but his father was also under oppression. Then Jesus revealed the truth: Graham's stepmother was herself filled with fear and was being controlled through fear by an abusive evil spirit. As Graham watched, the Lord drove out the spiritual forces of abuse, fear and control and his stepmother was suddenly softened. The fiery darts of her verbal abuse were quenched, and Jesus removed each one, breaking the power of the curses and speaking the blessing that He had wanted Graham to receive at that time.

The power of the fear and insecurities was broken and a deep peace quieted Graham's anxious heart. With this new perspective, Graham was able to forgive his stepmother and his father, and walk free. Today Graham is a very successful businessman who leads many to the Lord through his testimony of the practical, life-changing encounter with Christ that transformed his life.

Truth: Facing the Pain

Acknowledging your problems is the first step to overcoming them. These problems are keeping you from being all that you can be—all God intends for you to be. Look at Table 7B: Unhealthy Development and consider which adult behaviors and attitudes in your life may signal a problem rooted in this stage of your development.

Revelation: Revisiting the Scene

These problems need to be uprooted by the Lord. Ask the Holy Spirit to reveal where the problem began. He wants to do this for you: "You do not have, because you do not ask" (Jas. 4:2). As we seek His help, He is faithful to reveal how the whole mess started. Denial often protects us from remembering painful events that we were not able to cope with at the time; but at the right time the Holy Spirit helps us to remember the significant experiences. Ask Jesus to walk through this time with you.

Redemption: Healing and Deliverance

As we remember these experiences with the Lord, He reveals to us the Father caring for us and providing for our every need. When we have received healing, we often need new boundaries, which the Lord sets in place for us. As He re-parents us, He "corners" us (see Ps. 139:5) to redirect us on the right path; He sets boundaries and limits so that we will feel secure; and He imparts into our lives an ability to trust and a willingness to submit to His Lordship.

Restoration: The Planting of the Lord

As past hurts and wounds get healed and lies are uprooted, a planting of the Lord is put in their place. Our unmet needs are satisfied by the presence of the Lord, and a sense of peace and wholeness settles our anxious hearts. There is a tangible experience of healing and freedom as peace and confidence replace anxiety and insecurity.

Reparenting: Father God, "Father" Me

Once we have been set free, we face the challenge of learning to walk in new ways, according to God's Word. Scripture admonishes us, "work out your salvation with fear and trembling" (Phil. 2:12). What does that mean in concrete terms? It means learning to listen to and be taught by the Holy Spirit. It means learning to work out in our daily life the healing and deliverance the Lord has given us. It means humbling ourselves before God to acknowledge that we don't know how to live, and that we need to listen and obey as He teaches us how to live in freedom and wholeness according to His Word. In a very real way, Father God wants to teach us as a father teaches his child. Just as Jesus learned special obedience through the things He suffered, so also do we. Seeking Father God in the morning, opening our hearts to receive His instruction and committing ourselves to obey His directives will result in a day of walking in righteousness that pleases Him. Jesus is our model. He said, "I do nothing of my own but speak just what the Father has taught me" (John 8:28). Jesus always lived a life pleasing to the Father.

Along the way the Father may need to discipline us to break old destructive habits that were linked to our bondage and woundedness. He will begin to pry our fingers off these old habits and the survival mechanisms we used to try to make it on our own so that we can walk in greater freedom in Him. This fruit of change is always the evidence of what the Lord has done to set us free.

For some the change is instant and dramatic; for others it is a process yielding greater freedom over time. God restores us in the way He knows is best for each of us. We are unique and precious in His sight, and Father God restores us, individually, to His original intention.

THE FATHER'S HEALING PROCESS:
STEPS TO HEALING, FREEDOM AND RESTORATION

Healing

1. Identify the adult problems—behaviors and attitudes—that apply to you. (See Tables 7A/7B: Healthy/Unhealthy Development.)

2. Ask the Holy Spirit to reveal the root cause of each problem. The root is whatever happened to you during your early teens

that caused a wounding in your life and allowed the problem to take root. This revelation may be in the form of a memory, a picture, an impression, a thought, an awareness or some other way of "knowing" (see Luke 8:17).

3.   Ask Jesus to reveal His presence there with you. The presence of the Lord changes things (see Ps. 31:14-16; Heb. 13:5-6,8).

4.   Tell Jesus what you are feeling and thinking in this revealed time, place and experience. Listen to His response (see Pss. 88:1; 91:14-16).

5.   Ask Jesus to reveal what the Father intended for this time of your life. Jesus comes to show us the Father. Allow the Lord to minister to you; rest in Him and take time to receive what you need. He comes to care for your developmental needs, to heal you, to redeem all that was lost to you and to restore you to be all He created you to be (see Jer. 29:11; Matt. 15:13).

Freedom

6.   In the name of Jesus, break the power of the lie that was planted in your heart from the wound and ask the Lord to uproot it. Embrace the truth that has the power to set you free—the Word of God. Proclaim the promises in God's Word that are His answers to your need (see Matt. 15:13; John 8:31-32; 2 Cor. 1:20).

7.   Identify the patterns of sin, bondage or curses passed from generation to generation in your family. Break any generational curses, if necessary (see also Appendix A: Generational Curses). Forgive your parents and all those who wounded you (see Matt. 6:14; Gal. 3:13-14).

8.   Take authority, in Jesus' name, over any demonic oppression or influences in your life that the Lord has revealed. In the name of Jesus and His authority, command them to leave (see Luke 10:19; Jas. 4:7).

Restoration

9. Receive Father God as your eternal Father and receive your inheritance of life in Christ Jesus. Seek the Father each day to father you (see John 10:10; Heb. 12:10).

10. Ask the Holy Spirit to teach you how to walk in your "newness of life." Commit to listen to and obey the Holy Spirit. Begin to put God's specific Word for your need into action (see John 14:26; 16:13; Phil. 2:12-13).

Table 7A: Healthy Development

Stage of Life	Significant Issues	Developmental Task (needed for healthy development)	Adult Manifestation
12 Years to 13 Years	Time structuring Task priority Relationship skills Revisit in utero to 6 months issues	Refine, finalize, integrate in utero to 18 months resolutions Internalize appropriate time structures Internalize appropriate task priorities Learn to get needs met by asking Established order in life Explore social involvement	Appropriate in time management Able to prioritize tasks Healthy limits/ boundaries Godly order in life

Table 7A: Healthy Development (continued)

Stage of Life	Significant Issues	Developmental Task (needed for healthy development)	Adult Manifestation
14 Years	Thinking/ independence Anger Individuation Rebellion/ Opposition Test life values Revisit 2-year-old issues	Refine, finalize, integrate 2-year-old resolutions Final breaking of symbiosis: separation Finalize social contract Final incorporation of values Learn to manage anger in healthy way	Independent synergistic relationships Social contract guides interactions Accept responsibility for self Anger is managed constructively Integrity in real-life values

Table 7B: Unhealthy Development

Stage of Life	Significant Issues	Developmental Task (needed for healthy development)	Adult Manifestation
12 Years to 13 Years	Time structuring Task priority Relationship skills Revisit in utero to 18 months issues	In utero to 18 months tasks unresolved Incapacitate self with feelings Time structure lacking Lack of or insufficient boundaries	Insecurity with self and life Symbiotic/ unhealthy relationships Insecure with limits Problems staying on task

Table 7B: Unhealthy Development (continued)

Stage of Life	Significant Issues	Developmental Task (needed for healthy development)	Adult Manifestation
12 Years to 13 Years		Overprotected from natural consequences of behavior Hypocrisy	Addictive personality structure No godly order in life
14 Years	Thinking/ independence Anger Test life values Revisit 2-year-olds issues	2-year-olds tasks unresolved Discipline lacking Anger not confronted Limits and boundaries not enforced Dependency fostered Submission to control demanded Symbiosis reinforced Hypocrisy	Social contract weak or lacking Narcissistic; self-centered Control by domination, intimidation and/or manipulation Destructive competition Dependent on others Addictive personality structure Lack integrity in real-life values Control or resist new moves of God

8

DISCOVERING GOD-GIVEN DESTINY

Mid-Teens to Young Adult Years

EMMA'S STORY

Emma curled up in her bed and wept bitterly, bewildered at how this same nightmare could be happening again. She had trusted this woman friend—a Christian, she thought. Why was this happening to her? She never seemed to see the signs that danger was near.

This final phase of our development in the teen years is filled with challenge and the thrill of our growing independence. We tend to feel very grown up now and certain we can manage our life without any more help from our parents. Sex-role identification is being incorporated and integrated. Issues surrounding independence/dependence have been resolved and, having established our separation, we are psychologically ready to leave home. We are equipped to take full responsibility for our behavior.

This is also the time when we are refining and integrating professional and life skills to prepare for independent living. The light at the end of the tunnel is clearly visible and adolescent resolution is imminent. If all has gone well, we are able to integrate into a unified whole the resolutions of our earlier development with the relationship skills, independence, professional and life skills of adolescence, thus becoming a fully functioning, healthy individual. Unfortunately, for most of us, all has not gone well.

Adult Problems

Problems, at this stage of development, center in identity issues, especially sex-role identity and male/female relationships. Insecurity and unhealthy dependency can give rise to symbiotic relationships instead of the desired separation, independence and development of personal responsibility. Sex-role confusion undermines confidence and security in knowing how to be and behave appropriately. The resurgence of wounds from our early development complicates matters as well. Tendencies toward legalism and battling real or imagined injustices can also put stress on relationships with others. These problems cause serious disabilities in being able to function as a mature adult in society and greatly hinder fulfilling our destiny in the kingdom of God. Let's consider what should have happened during these years to prepare us for the plan God has for our lives.

Developmental Process

The storms of negativity have passed and we sail into relatively tranquil waters in this next stage of development. We are a bit calmer and find it easier to flow in cooperation with parents and family. We are taking more responsibility for our life and preparing for eventual separation from our family to become an independent, responsible individual in society.

Developmental Needs: Fifteen Years Old

Sex-role Identification

Sex-role identity becomes our focus. The inevitable "why?" is back, as we revisit the three- to five-year-old stage to settle any unfinished business. This time our why is a social why: "Why can't I?" "Why won't you let me?" "Why don't you trust me?" and so on.

Fear and righteousness are recurring themes as we reprocess old stuff once more. We have many questions regarding male/female relationships and a desire to know about our parents' social history. In order to confidently embrace our identity as a man or woman and acknowledge that it is good to be who God made us to be, we need parental guidance and healthy role models.

Daughters are attentive to fathers now and need fatherly love to develop a healthy self-image as a woman. Fathers need to give daughters affirmation and protection to communicate how valuable they are. Through a healthy relationship with her father, a daughter learns to expect to be treated with love and respect as the woman of God that she is. Sons are attentive to mothers and need to receive permission and encouragement to grow up and become independent. It is also important for mothers to affirm their sons in developing responsibility. This then gives the son the release from mother without fear of hurting her. It frees him to become the godly man he is destined to be.[1]

Developmental Needs: Sixteen to Thirty Years Old

Separation and Independence

Yes, 16 to 30. Current research indicates that due to the highly technological society in which we live, training for professions now takes much longer and can cause a young person to remain economically dependent for a longer period, even up to 30 years of age.

This was a great encouragement to a pastor at one of our seminars recently. He came up afterwards to tell us what a relief it was to know that his son was normal. His son had left home three times to live on his own, and for various reasons had ended up back home again. But since he was not yet 30, he was still in the normal range of development. Now he was preparing to leave home again, hopefully for the last time. Hallelujah!

Separation and independence are important for us in these closing years of adolescence. We need to function independently and take personal responsibility for ourselves. Leftover issues from the six- to twelve-year-old period will surface again to be resolved, especially issues of injustice. It is a time when we look back and reflect on the successes and failures of the past, as well as look forward and plan for the future. It is time to begin the transition and prepare to leave home. Parents need to support us by letting go and being available for consultation as needed. We need to take charge of our life and begin to move out into the world.[2] We need to receive the blessing of our parents and be released back to our eternal Father God to serve Him with our life.

Decisions About Life and Self

What happens to us in these closing years of adolescence either enhances or diminishes our self-confidence as an adult. The major issues for us now are: It is good to be male/female; I can/can't handle responsibility.

Weeds and Roots

The wounds we suffer in our mid- to late-teens transfer immediately into our adult life. Sex-role confusion, symbiotic relationships and an inordinate sensitivity to unrighteousness and injustice are the most common problems rooted in this stage of development.

Sex-role Confusion

Sex-role confusion is fairly common in the wake of the feminist movement and the blurring of the differences between men and women in modern Western culture. Simply defined, it is a lack of security in sexual identity—not knowing what it means to be a healthy man or woman. This insecurity can be slight or severe, depending on what has happened in the earlier stages of a person's life. The absence of a father or mother can leave an individual without a role model for his or her sexual identity; or to a much more serious degree, sexual abuse or exploitation in the teen years can cause confusion or revulsion of sexual identity. In cases where there has been a history of sexual perversion in the family for generations, there is an even greater risk. A family history of sexual perversion creates a demonic stronghold that causes vulnerability to a broad spectrum of sexual perversions, including homosexuality.

If you suffer from sex-role confusion, the important thing to realize is that these wounds can be healed and you can be restored to wholeness. The Father has made a way.

EMMA'S STORY (CONTINUED)

Emma, in her late forties, had allowed a lady friend who seemed like a lovely Christian to move in to share her home. It was only after the woman had been there for some months that the relationship began to change. Emma found herself more and more controlled by her housemate and, not wanting to cause friction, she submitted. It wasn't long before she felt like a prisoner in her own home. To make matters worse, this lady was into strange "spiritual activities." Emma wanted her out but felt trapped.

Symbiotic Relationships

Insecurity leads to symbiotic relationships. If people are unable to manage their feelings or are incapable of thinking and solving problems on their own, they become vulnerable to symbiotic relationships, which are based on an unhealthy dependency on others. They relinquish responsibility for these areas to someone else. In effect, they give others control of their life and expect them to manage all or parts of it for them. This often turns into a double-edged sword; although they want to be taken care of, at the same time they resent the control. They can become passive-aggressive and vindictive. Most often this happens because people were smothered and controlled during key stages of their development and not allowed or encouraged to become responsible for their lives.

Overprotective parents who shield their children from the invaluable learning experiences of natural consequences do them a great disservice. They leave their children with the impression that "I am not capable. I am not responsible. I am simply helpless"—and it is very scary to feel helpless in the world. Helplessness can pave the way for addiction. Even people who are quite intelligent and capable will sometimes become addicts to sabotage their success and maintain their belief that they are helpless and incapable.

AARON'S STORY

Aaron was out with his friends at a popular teen hangout one Friday night when one of the kids in the group got the brilliant idea that it would be great fun to "bolt" (i.e., leave without paying for the food they had eaten), which is what they did. However, the next day, the owner, who knew Aaron, called his home. I was sitting in their kitchen at the time the call came. Lara, his mother, was so embarrassed and upset that she told the man she would come right away and pay the bill. "Wait a minute," I said. "Whose responsibility is this?" After she calmed down, she realized Aaron needed to go and pay the bill and apologize to the owner. It is an awful feeling to get caught doing something wrong, but facing the consequences of our behavior is what builds character. Needless to say, having to face the owner and ask forgiveness, and pay the entire bill, left a lasting impression on Aaron, which will ensure he never does that again!

Dealing with the natural consequences of our actions is the stuff of character building and growth in being responsible. I also personally believe it is the grace of God in our lives to keep us on track.

Father God's Intervention
EMMA'S STORY (CONTINUED)

Emma was quite ill when she came for prayer. She thought she was going insane but, in fact, she was under an attack of witchcraft. When we prayed, the Lord revealed the truth. This woman she had invited to live in her home was not a Christian and was in fact operating in the occult. As we came into agreement in the name of Jesus, the power of the witchcraft was broken, the heaviness and oppression lifted and Emma was free.

We asked the Lord to reveal the root of this destructive cycle in which Emma had continuously found herself, trusting blindly and always getting hurt. The Lord gave Emma a picture of her mother constantly hovering over her, controlling her every move even into her teen years. Her mom was so strong that Emma just submitted, not feeling strong enough to take her mother on and fight for her freedom. She opted for peace at all costs.

In the long run, the cost was too high. In submitting to the control of her mother, she came under the oppression of the spirit of control and, to make matters worse, she was also under the fear of man. The Lord revealed the picture of Emma all tied up and blindfolded. She wanted to be free and asked the Lord to come to her. He removed the blindfold and cut off the ropes binding her. It was time to leave her father's house and become independent. She broke the symbiotic tie with her mother and commanded the fear of man and the spirit of control out of her life. Finally, she stood against the witchcraft, commanding it out of her life, in Jesus' name. She went home armed for battle to get the woman out, only to find that as she had committed herself to the Lord, the enemy had fled before her. The woman and all her belongings were gone without a trace. Now Emma, submitted to the Lord and under His protection, never makes a serious decision without asking her First Love, her Redeemer King, who watches over her life. She is safe in the secret place; her life is hidden in Christ and in God.

Truth: Facing the Pain

We all have problems, shortcomings or hang-ups in our life. It is no shame to have needs—but it would be a terrible shame to allow them to continue to hinder you from becoming all that God created you to be. Review Table 8: Healthy/Unhealthy Development to see if there are any adult problems that relate to this stage of development in your life. No matter what binds you, Jesus can set you free. What the Lord reveals, He heals.

Revelation: Revisiting the Scene

The Holy Spirit is the revealer of truth. Sometimes we don't see the cause of our problems clearly; we don't recognize the connections of certain early experiences with the trouble in our life today. We need the Holy Spirit to reveal the root cause and its connection to the challenge in our present life. Walk through the revelation with Jesus. He knows how to make you whole again.

Redemption: Healing and Deliverance

Jesus comes to reveal the Father. He sees the destruction planted in our lives and He uproots it. Jesus redeems us and prepares us for the process of restoration.

The Father created you as a man or woman according to His perfect plan for your life. Security in your identity is critical to becoming all that the Father created you to be. Allow the Father to provide the support, protection, healing and restoration you need to be free.

We all need to become independent and confident in our abilities to make it in life. Father God wants to give you the support and encouragement He knows you need. He wants to free you from the struggles of immaturity, the pain of addiction, the bondage of controlling symbiotic relationships. He wants to restore your gifts and callings, give you healthy life-giving relationships, eternal destiny, purpose and freedom so that you can continue to mature and become more and more like Jesus.

Restoration: The Planting of the Lord

The Father restores and supernaturally imparts into your life your true identity in Him. He wants to restore your healthy self-image. He wants you to see yourself as He sees you and be secure in your uniqueness. There are "Deborahs" and there are "Ruths"; there are "Davids" and there are "Peters": all godly in their being, yet all unique and different from one another in their manly and womanly expression. Let the Lord restore your identity in Him.

The Father also wants to restore your destiny—the gifts and callings you were born to fulfill in His kingdom. It is time to dream again; it is time to dream the Father's dream for your life.

Reparenting: Father God, "Father" Me

The Father waits to meet you every morning. He longs to nurture you, teach you, train you and bring you into maturity. Jesus is our role model. All that we have missed out on in our lives, we can learn from His life and from fellowship with Him. As we grow in godly maturity, the Father can release greater spiritual authority to us by His Spirit and together we can become the glorious Church, the radiant Bride of Christ that we are meant to be: "A planting of the LORD for the display of his splendor" (Isa. 61:3).

THE FATHER'S HEALING PROCESS:
STEPS TO HEALING, FREEDOM AND RESTORATION

Healing

1. Identify the adult problems—behaviors or attitudes that apply to you. (See Tables 8A/8B: Healthy/Unhealthy Development.)

2. Ask the Holy Spirit to reveal the root cause of each problem. The root is whatever happened to you during your late teens and early adulthood that caused a wounding in your life and allowed the problem to take root. This revelation may be in the form of a memory, a picture, an impression, a thought, an awareness or some other way of "knowing" (see Luke 8:17).

3. Ask Jesus to reveal His presence there with you. The presence of the Lord changes things (see Ps. 31:14-16; Heb. 13:5-6,8).

4. Tell Jesus what you are feeling and thinking in this revealed time, place, experience. Listen to His response (see Pss. 88:1; 91:14-16).

5. Ask Jesus to reveal what the Father intended for this time of your life. Jesus comes to show us the Father. Allow the Lord to minister to you; rest in Him and take time to receive what you need. He comes to care for your developmental needs, to heal you, to redeem all that was lost to you and to restore you to be all He created you to be (see Jer. 29:11; Matt. 15:13).

Freedom

6. In the name of Jesus, break the power of the lie that was planted in your heart from the wound and ask the Lord to uproot it.

Embrace the truth—the Word of God—that has the power to set you free. Proclaim the promises in God's Word that are His answers to your need (see Matt. 15:13; John 8:31-32; 2 Cor. 1:20).

7. Identify the patterns of sin, bondage or curses passed from generation to generation in your family. Break any generational curses, if necessary (see also Appendix A: Generational Curses). Forgive your parents and all those who wounded you (see Matt. 6:14; Gal. 3:13-14).

8. Take authority, in Jesus' name, over any demonic oppression or influences in your life that the Lord has revealed. In the name of Jesus and His authority, command them to leave (see Luke 10:19; Jas. 4:7).

Restoration

9. Receive Father God as your eternal Father and receive your inheritance of life in Christ Jesus. Seek the Father each day to father you (see John 10:10; Heb. 12:10).

10. Ask the Holy Spirit to teach you how to walk in your "newness of life." Commit to listen to and obey the Holy Spirit and begin to put God's Word into action in your life (see John 14:26; 16:13; Phil. 2:12-13).

Table 8A: Healthy Development

Stage of Life	Significant Issues	Developmental Task (needed for healthy development)	Adult Manifestation
15 Years	Identity: sex-role identification

Acculturation

Relationship skills | Refine, finalize, integrate 3- to 5-year-old resolutions

Incorporate sex-role identity in relationships | Secure in identity

Effective relationship skills

Operate in grace and mercy of God |

Table 8A: Healthy Development (continued)

Stage of Life	Significant Issues	Developmental Task (needed for healthy development)	Adult Manifestation
15 Years	Revisit 3- to 5-year-old issues	Incorporate personal identity Incorporate cultural identity	
16 Years to 30 Years	Revisit 6- to 12-year-old issues Professional/ personal/ relationship skill development and integration Adolescent Resolution	Refine, finalize, integrate 6- to 12-year-old resolutions Establish professional/ occupational skills/life skills Independent/ dependent struggle resolved	Develop skills in profession/ occupation Develop relationship skills Maintain healthy balance between responsibilities and relationships Train and mentor others Dynamic, continuous growth toward maturity Continue to mature in the Lord

Table 8B: Unhealthy Development

Stage of Life	Significant Issues	Developmental Task (needed for healthy development)	Adult Manifestation
15 Years	Identity: Sex-role identification Acculturation Revisit 3- to 5-year-old issues	3- to 5-year-old tasks unresolved Sexual exploitation/ abuse Physical/ emotional abuse Unhealthy or unrighteous role models Consistent failure in relationships Reinforce inappropriate sex-role identification Hypocrisy	Lack real life values Insecure in identity Insecure and/or confused sex-role identity Socially inept Addictive personality structure Insecure in identity in Christ Bound by religious tradition Function legalistically
16 Years to 30 Years	Skill development/ integration Adolescent resolution Revisit 6- to 12-year-old issues	6- to 12-year-old tasks unresolved Independence discouraged Control/inhibit separation/ independence Skill learning not provided or encouraged Hypocrisy	Struggle with 6- to 12-year-old issues Struggle with immaturity Rigid and inflexible Passive-aggressive behavior Activities exclude opposite sex Addictive personality structure Lack God's vision for life

9

NATURAL DEVELOPMENT AND SPIRITUAL DEVELOPMENT
The Process and Influences

The spiritual did not come first, but the natural, and after that the spiritual.
1 CORINTHIANS 15:46

Our natural development affects our spiritual development. At whatever stage our natural development went well, our spiritual development was easier. But at the stages in which we had problems in our natural development, we struggled in our spiritual development. What a motivation to pursue healing! Healing from the Lord—receiving what we needed at each stage of development—frees us to grow in our relationship with the Lord and progress in our spiritual maturity. Let's explore this thought a bit more in detail.

Natural Development and Spiritual Development
It is significant to note that the human development stages we go through, from the womb through adolescence, are the very same stages all people progress through after being born again in the Spirit (see 1 Pet. 2:2). In fact, our spiritual development advances through the very same stages we all go through in our natural, human development.[1] These stages, both human and spiritual, are similar in every way, with one exception: In our spiritual development, we have a perfect parent caring for us, Father God.

Let's briefly consider the comparison of the two developmental processes from birth through adolescence.

Birth to Six Months

Birth to six months is basically the stage at which we are cared for unconditionally. We don't do much except exist and receive care. Mom just seems to know what we need, and she responds. What a great life for us! In this way we are affirmed in our existence and develop basic trust and security.

When we are born again, there is a birth-to-six-months stage in the Lord. This stage may last for more than six months, maybe for a year. During this time, God just seems to pour out His provision, care and blessings upon us unconditionally. Remember? You needed something and God just provided. You didn't have to pray, travail or fast for weeks to receive. During this early stage, God affirms our existence and encourages our trust in Him as a child of God. He's there immediately when there is a need. I have experienced God's abundant provision during this early developmental stage in Him—for myself and in the lives of other new believers over the years.

When I (Frank) was first born again, I remember thinking one day that I needed $100 for a bill I had to pay. I didn't know where I was going to get the money. I don't think I even spent time to pray about it. I just needed it and that was it. I went to bed, got up the next morning, went to the drawer to get out a pair of socks and under the pair of socks was, yep, you guessed it, $100. Now, I know I didn't put that $100 there. No one else did either. God did it. I didn't travail for weeks in prayer for the $100. I had the need, I thought about it, my Father in heaven saw the need and He met it. This is how it goes for this newborn time in the Lord, the first months after being born again.

Father God wants us to know that we can trust Him completely. Trust is the foundation of our relationship with the Lord and the bedrock for our faith to develop. Without this security, our walk with the Lord will be a struggle. We must have this trust in God restored in our life to move forward in maturity.

Six to 18 Months: Exploration

The 6- to 18-months stage in our natural development is the active, exploration stage. We come alive with motivation, initiative, creativity and mobility. We energize to explore the world around us.

So it is when we are at the 6- to 18-months stage in the Lord. We are excited about the things of God. We talk to people about Jesus, and they come to the Lord. WOW, we have an evangelistic ministry! We consume the Bible and spend much time studying God's Word, thrilled about what we are discovering. We learn about casting out demons, in Jesus' name, and when we do it, demons flee. WOW, we have a deliverance ministry! We read about laying hands on people for healing, so we lay hands on someone with a headache and it immediately goes away. WOW, we have a healing ministry! We go from one end of our town to the other ministering to people, and things happen. Wow, let's go clean out the hospitals! Let's go to the funeral parlors and raise the dead!

It has been said, in some church circles, that born-again believers need to be restrained for the first 18 months of their born-again lives. I don't think so. This is the time when God allows us to explore the things of the Kingdom. He, I believe, is very pleased when we are bursting to discover and test out our new life in God. I think about the things I did those first couple of years in the Lord. Now I wonder how my family and close friends survived that time with me. I did some really crazy things in this time of exploration. Maybe you didn't, but I know many people who did do things they would not do today. With childlike abandon we try out everything we discover in God's Word, and we have some amazing experiences. Through it all we learn and grow. And God delights in us.

Being inhibited by the fear and oppressive control of parents in this stage makes it difficult to hear God's voice and be free in the Lord in later life. These spiritual forces put us in bondage. The Lord needs to revisit those early experiences with you to put things right so you can be free to hear His voice and follow His plan for your life.

Two Years: Beginning Independence

Until now our spiritual development has been blissfully unhindered. Then one day we go to lay hands on someone and we hear, in our hearts, "No!" You go to do it again and you hear, "No!" once again. (*Hmmm.*) "I rebuke you, Satan!" God says, "I'm not Satan!" "God, let me lay hands on this person! I have the healing heat of the Holy Spirit flowing in my hands. All I need to do is lay hands on this person and he'll be healed. God, I'm doing it for You!" Again, you go to do it and you again hear, "NO!" "God, why not?" And God says, "Now is the time to learn obedience because, son (daughter), without obedience, you're of no use to me." You are entering the two-year-old stage with Father God.

The two-year-old stage of human development is the time when we receive discipline, learn obedience, are taught to cooperate with others, and come out of the self-centered approach to life. The born-again Christian will also go through a two-year-old stage in his or her spiritual development with God. Giving up control, learning to hear and obey the voice of the Lord, taking personal responsibility for our actions and learning submission to Jesus as Lord, and those in authority over us, are all goals for this time in our spiritual development. However, if we have unresolved two-year-old issues, we will have trouble letting go of control and the need to have things our own way. Conflict, competition and control can block us from God's plan for our lives. More than any other stage of development, this one seems to be a stumbling block for many people.

Three to Five Years: Identity

Identity is the focus in this stage of human development. Who am I in my family, in my community, in my culture? Not everything we learned about our identity in our natural development is true for our spiritual development. The culture of the Kingdom is often at odds with the cultures we grew up in. So we have some work to do with the Lord to renew our minds and be transformed (see Rom. 12:2). The truth we find in God's Word challenges what we thought was true, and we have lots of questions. Who am I as a child of God, in the family of God, in the Kingdom? Just like in natural development, information gathering to learn how to be and what to do is important in our spiritual development.

In many ways, we are conformed to this world. Our culture is our way of life, our beliefs, our traditions. If we don't know who we are, how can we be who God intended us to be in this world and fulfill our purpose? Jesus wants to transform us so we can express

His image through our true identity—who He made us to be. In this stage, we begin to live what Jesus modeled for us in His Word. Much like children playing dress-up, we are practicing to be like Jesus. Scripture comes alive to us and we begin to learn how things work in the kingdom of God. The power of the Word is in doing it. We don't always get it right. But we learn important lessons that move us forward in our quest for maturity.

Six to 12 Years: Gifts and Callings

In our maturing process we are now discovering our skills and developing the gifts God has given us. We begin to dream God's dream for our life. (What do I want to be when I grow up? I want to be a doctor, pastor, policeman, missionary, astronaut.) These are the seeds of God's calling on our life. What we imagined our future would be when we were children may be far less than what God has planned.

Frank wanted to be a Catholic priest. He was raised in an Italian Catholic family. The priests were highly respected and had great influence in the families. When the priest came for a visit, everyone was on his or her best behavior. Frank was very impressed with the positive effect priests had on families. So he was going to be a priest. Until he started high school and discovered . . . girls. Catholic priest? No. Years later, Frank had an encounter with the Lord and was born again and filled with the Spirit. We were led to embrace the larger Body of Christ and serve in various communities of faith. After many years of faithfulness in small things, Frank was living the dream God had for his life: not a priest serving a small community, but a *New Testament* priest sent to the nations.

What dream did you have as a child? In that dream are the seeds of what God is doing or wants to do in your life. If you don't remember, ask Him. The Father never forgets. It is never too late. We don't have to make it happen. Our responsibility is to listen and take the steps of obedience, and God will bring it to pass.

Teen Years: Going on to Maturity

In this stage, the Holy Spirit has been moving among us, stirring up a desire for greater intimacy with the Lord. The mystery of the Bride and the Bridegroom is being revealed in greater measure. If we are honest, we will admit that relationship is the challenge of our life. Stop for a moment and consider: Do you have more problems in your profession or in your relationships? Most of us would have to say relationships. One reason is that our culture is a task-oriented culture. Performance is a high priority and defines us all too often. Biblical maturity is reaching the "whole measure of the fullness of Christ" (Eph. 4:13). The heartbeat of the Lord is relationship. He came and died for us to restore our relationship to the Father.

In the teen years, relationship is the most important skill being developed. So why do so many of us struggle in relationship with ourselves, with others and with God? In our brokenness, we are not able to really develop life-giving relationships. That is why healing your past life is so important.

At whatever stage of development you have been wounded and hung up in your growth because of past wounds, you will experience difficulty in your walk with Father God. This is a developmental fact, which we have experienced in our own lives and in the lives of all those we have ministered to over the years. When people have past developmental wounds, they experience arrested growth and become hung up at the earlier stage or stages of development where the wound or wounds occurred. They are unable to fully mature because of the past wound that is crippling and preventing them from reaching the fullness of what God wants for their life. They become unable to fulfill their God-given destiny. For this reason, we believe God wants us to deal with the wounds in our lives, with Him, so that we can continue to grow and mature in the Lord and fulfill the destiny He has given to each of us.

Jesus is seeking a Bride to stand beside Him to rule and reign with Him in the earth. He told us the kingdom of God is within us. As we mature and become more like Jesus, we can be aware of His presence within us and consciously carry His presence everywhere we go.

Jesus is the full expression of the kingdom of God. In Him is the answer for every need. It is "Christ in you, the hope of glory" (Col. 1:27). So let's heed the call of the Spirit of God and go on to maturity.

APPENDIX A

GENERATIONAL CURSES

Breaking the Inheritance of Destruction

It is time to awaken from our sleep of complacency. It is time to realize that the fullness of our inheritance has been stolen by the enemy. The Lord does not want us to be ignorant of Satan's schemes (see 2 Cor. 2:11).

One major strategy of the enemy is to take whole families captive through generational curses and bondages. Once the enemy gets into a family, he begins to build a stronghold over their minds and hearts. The Greek word for "stronghold," as used in 2 Corinthians 10:4, is *ochuros* and means "a hard place." It refers to a place on the battlefield that is an entrenchment or a fortress. As a verb it means "to fortify" or "make firm" and is used both literally and figuratively. Generational curses and bondages are strongholds of the enemy in us that we inherit from our forefathers. Just as we inherit physical characteristics from our ancestors, so too we receive a spiritual inheritance of blessings and curses. For the blessings, we can be truly thankful. The curses need to be broken.

It will be important to consider certain aspects of this biblical truth in order to grasp fully what generational curses and bondages are and, most importantly, how to break them in our lives and in the lives of our children. Here's what Scripture tells us:

> The LORD is longsuffering, and of great mercy, forgiving iniquity and transgression, and by no means clearing the guilty, visiting the iniquity of the fathers upon the children unto the third and fourth generation (Num. 14:18, *KJV*).

It is clear from this Scripture that iniquity in past generations opens a door to the enemy and gives him legal access into the family to oppress the children to the third and fourth generation. This opening into a person's life, which he or she may or may not be aware of, allows demonic oppression to operate covertly and cause havoc. Generational curses and bondages are the result of sin (see Exod. 20:5), a lack of knowledge (see Hos. 4:6), or a family history of life without God (see Eph. 2:12). The curses and bondages are then passed on as an inheritance from generation to generation until they are broken by the power of the blood of Jesus.

Recognizing and acknowledging generational curses and bondages is the first step to freedom. Whenever problems have a generational root, certain characteristics are discernible. A person in bondage to a particular sin or destructive pattern of behavior, emotion or thought feels powerless and driven by compulsions, even though he or she is desperate to be free, and truly repents. They are often tormented by guilt and condemnation and feel trapped or enslaved by their vulnerability or oppression.

Another indicator is when a person is vulnerable to being victimized by the sin of others, as in the case of abuse, and there is also evidence of the sin, curse or bondage in past generations. In such cases, a person can look back and detect a similar pattern in his or her parents and other family members over the generations.

The destruction, devastation and death brought on by generational curses and bondages are staggering. Because the degree of destruction does not remain the same but rather increases exponentially from generation to generation, annihilation is its ultimate end—the third and fourth generations are being targeted for destruction by the enemy. Demonic manifestations may occur if the enemy is firmly entrenched over three or four generations, and those in bondage can be under strong deception and spiritual blindness, unable to see the truth or receive correction until the curse and bondage is broken.

The good news is that "the curse causeless shall not come" (Prov. 26:2, *KJV*). The devil has no power without permission or a legal opening into our lives. If great-grandma let him in, you can kick him out and shut the door.

> Christ redeemed us from the curse of the law by becoming a curse for us (Gal. 3:13).

Jesus Himself said:

> I have given you authority to trample on snakes and scorpions and to overcome all the power of the enemy; nothing will harm you (Luke 10:19).

Jesus went to the cross not only to save us from eternal separation from God but also to redeem our families from the curse of the law. Once we have received revelation, knowledge of our need, and we humble ourselves before God, He will redeem us and set us free from the curses and bondages inherited through our natural bloodline. In exchange, we will receive an eternal inheritance of life and peace through Christ Jesus.

The prophet Daniel received revelation of the sins of his forefathers that hindered the Israelites from returning to the Promised Land. As he humbled himself and stood in the gap to ask the Lord to forgive the sins of his forefathers, the bondage was broken and Israel was set free (see Dan. 9:1-6).

Today is the day of salvation. Today is the day to set ourselves and our children free. The Lord has made a way.

> Know therefore that the Lord your God is God; he is the faithful God, keeping his covenant of love to a thousand generations of those who love him and keep his commands (Deut. 7:9).

It is time to reclaim our lost inheritance in the kingdom of God. Jesus still comes to set the captives free.

Causes of Generational Curses

Simply stated, a generational curse is a breach in a person's life. He or she may or may not be aware of the breach. This opening, which may take the form of actual curses, sins or bondages, gives access for demonic oppression to operate undercover and cause havoc in a person's life.

Iniquity and Sin

"The LORD is longsuffering, and of great mercy, forgiving iniquity and transgression, and by no means clearing the guilty, visiting the iniquity of the fathers upon the children unto the third and fourth generation" (Num. 14:18, *KJV*).

Lack of Knowledge

"My people are destroyed from lack of knowledge. Because you have rejected knowledge, I also reject you . . . because you have ignored the law of your God, I also will ignore your children" (Hos. 4:6).

Family History of Life Without God

"Remember that at that time you were separate from Christ . . . foreigners to the covenants of the promise, without hope and without God in the world" (Eph. 2:12).

One thing is for sure, there has to be a cause if the person is a Christian. "The curse causeless shall not come" (Prov. 26:2, *KJV*). Most important, there is a way to break a generational curse. What the Lord reveals, He heals. "Christ redeemed us from the curse of the law by becoming a curse for us, for it is written: 'Cursed is everyone who is hung on a tree.' He redeemed us in order that the blessing given to Abraham might come to the Gentiles through Christ Jesus, so that by faith we might receive the promise of the Spirit" (Gal. 3:13-14).

How to Break Generational Curses and Bondages

- *Identify the generational sins, curses and bondages in your family.* Ask the Holy Spirit to reveal the hidden ones (see Matt. 10:26; Luke 8:17; 12:2). Ask the Lord to forgive the specific sins of the past generations that have been revealed by the Holy Spirit. If you personally have committed the sin, repent and receive forgiveness (see Dan. 9:1-6; 1 John 1:9).

- *Break all curses, bondages and demonic strongholds in the name and authority of Jesus Christ* (see Luke 10:19; 2 Cor. 10:4).

- *Receive freedom from the curse through Jesus Christ* (see Gal. 3:13-14; 1 Pet. 1:18-19).

- *Release your children from the curse and any effects of it.* Establish Father God's legacy for your family, namely "blessings for a thousand generations."

- *Proclaim the blessings of Deuteronomy 28:1-14 over yourself and your children* (see Exod. 20:6; Lev. 26:39-45; Deut. 7:9; 28:1-14).

CONTROL BRINGS LIFE OR BRINGS DEATH

During the past several years, much has been written on the destructive nature of control. We have also been fighting the battle to reveal the devastating results that control brings into the lives of people, organizations and cultures. This appendix contains some of our research, revelation and findings on control.

There are various forms of control:

- *Self-control:* a fruit of the Holy Spirit;

- *God-given control:* given to individuals, leaders and authority figures for the process of carrying out dominion, rightful authority and responsibility in areas under their charge. This type of control takes the form of leading, guiding and directing. It brings order, focus, clarity, safety and discipline. The results of this type of control are the following: brings life, health, growth and freedom to individuals, relationships, organizations and cultures;

- *Quality control:* assures that products produced are of high quality.

In addition, there is the type of control on which we will focus:

- *Negative control:* used by man to fulfill the goal of maintaining power and influence over individuals or people groups. The intent is to pressure individuals, organizations or cultures to accomplish self-seeking, arbitrarily established sets of desired results. This form of control is rooted in fear. Since our God has not given us a spirit of fear, this form of control is motivated by Satan. It is manifested in domination, manipulation and intimidation, and its results are negative, bringing death, destruction and bondage to people, relationships, organizations and cultures.

The first three types of control—self-control, God-given control and quality control—are developmentally healthy. They result in healthy growth and maturity. They breed independently responsible people and ensure personal rights and freedom. The last form of control is developmentally destructive. It results in arrested growth and immaturity and breeds dependency on the controlling agent, ensuring the obstruction of personal rights and placing others in bondage.

Most dictionaries include, among their other definitions of "control," one similar to the following: "A personality or spirit believed to activate the utterances or performances of a spiritualist medium." In our view, this definition cuts to the very heart of negative control. Control is so destructive because it is not a personality characteristic or trait but a spirit. This type of control manifests itself in three ways: *intimidation, domination, manipulation.*

There is nothing good about this form of control. It is motivated by fear, having been initially learned in the symbiosis stage and incorporated by the developing person for the purpose of survival. When an infant is controlled by caretakers from birth, he or she learns that control is the only acceptable way to get needs met to survive. In the beginning, control causes the newborn baby to incorporate fear in the form of not having his or her survival needs met unconditionally. Fear then becomes the motivation behind incorporating control as an approach to the world to get the needs for survival met. Once this spiritual force takes hold, it becomes the primary way in which an individual ensures that his or her needs, wants, desires and goals in life are satisfied and fulfilled.

This control has the following results:

- It builds weakness in the one using it because it reinforces dependence on the use of external forces and factors to get things done.

- It builds weakness in the person being controlled, stunting the development of independent reasoning, growth, self-discipline and self-control, which is a fruit of the Spirit.

- It builds weakness within the relationship in which it is being exerted.[1]

Because fear is the motivation behind this spiritual force, fear replaces cooperation, causing the people who are interacting to become arbitrary, at odds with each other (adversarial), competitive and defensive.

In addition, where the spirit of control is in operation there usually exists a counter spiritual force: rebellion. Wherever you find control, you will eventually find rebellion. The reverse is also true. Wherever you find rebellion, the oppression of control is either in operation or once was in operation in the person's life.

We believe that people use control because they do not know any other way to get a job done or ensure that their needs are met. Control is addictive. When it works one time, it is used as a behavior of choice to fulfill needs, wants and desires. All of us learn control from the way our parents handled us and our needs during infancy and childhood. This form of control is very often generational, handed down from generation to generation. It must be dealt with not only in the person's life in the present, but in the past generations as well.

We see so many infants who are being raised under this form of control. In the scope of our ministry, we are confronted again and again by its destructive results.

In 2 Corinthians 5:14 we are told, "For the love of Christ controls us" (*NASB*). Here we see a biblical principle for relationship, which makes a clear link between love and control. When the love of others and their love of us "controls" our relationships, molding us and leading us, the result will be healthy, desirable benefits and outcomes. When the main ingredient of love is missing from the equation, then we must realize that control becomes an entity in and of itself. Control becomes the ultimate force that drives us to satisfy our needs, fulfill our desires and accomplish our goals.

We learn in 1 John 4:18 that when love exists, fear does not. In fact, "perfect love casts out fear" (*NKJV*). Again, the foundation is fear. If fear is cast out because love exists, then there is no motivation for control and, thus, no need to control. We then come back to 2 Corinthians 5:14 and will choose to walk in the reality of 2 Timothy 1:7: "For God did not give us a spirit of timidity, but a spirit of power, of love and of self-discipline."

As we have already established, the foundation and motivation behind this form of control is fear. When a situation arises that causes fear and the individual does not deal with it in prayer, asking the Holy Spirit for direction and guidance, he or she risks getting into self-designed methods to find a solution. These self-designed methods replace Holy Spirit-initiated action and thus can only be empowered and maintained by human effort. The energy for this human effort is sustained by control because the person has not submitted to the Holy Spirit, who now steps aside. Control is now free to take over as the motivating force behind the individual's feeling, thinking and doing. Control takes the place of the Holy Spirit in a person's life and becomes lord, with the destructive outcomes previously listed. This is truly a tool of the enemy designed to torment and destroy Christians and non-Christians alike.

We believe that the Lord recognizes and understands how people get into this form of control. He does not condemn us for this, but He does expect us to get out of it as soon as we recognize what has happened.

To understand more about this type of control, we encourage you to attend one of the many seminars we conduct on God's Plan for Human Development, in which we deal with the issue of control—its origins, motivations and outcomes—and specifically minister into this destructive aspect of human interaction.

BIBLIOGRAPHY

Armstrong, Thomas. *The Myth of the ADD Child: 50 Ways to Improve Your Child's Behavior and Attention Span Without Drugs, Labels, or Coercion.* New York: Penguin Group Publishing, 1997.

Blankeslee, Sandra. "New Connections: When It's Time to Make Changes in Your Life, What Role Does Your Brain Play?" *American Health.* March 1990.

Dobbins, Richard D. *Venturing into a Child's World.* Akron, OH: Emerge Ministries, Inc., 1985.

——— . *Venturing Into a Teenager's World.* Akron, OH: Emerge Ministries, Inc., 1987.

Elkind, David. *A Sympathetic Understanding of the Child: Birth to Sixteen*, 3rd edition. Needham Heights, MA: Allyn and Bacon/Paramount Publishing, 1994.

——— . *All Grown Up and No Place to Go: Teenagers in Crisis.* New York: Addison-Wesley Publishing Co., 1984.

——— . *Miseducation: Preschoolers at Risk.* New York: Alfred A. Knopf Inc., 1987.

——— . *The Hurried Child: Growing Up Too Fast Too Soon.* New York: Addison-Wesley Publishing Co., 1988.

Erikson, Erik H. *Childhood and Society.* New York: W.W. Norton & Co. Inc., 1963.

Gibbs, Nancy. "The EQ Factor: New Brain Research Suggests That Emotions Not IQ May Be the True Measure of Human Intelligence," *Time Magazine*, October 1995.

Ingelman-Sundberg, A. *A Child Is Born.* New York: Dell Publishing Co., 1979.

Levin, Pamela. *Cycles of Power: A User's Guide to the Seven Seasons of Life.* Deerfield Beach, FL: Health Communications, 1988.

MacNutt, Frances and Judith. *Praying for Your Unborn Child.* New York: Doubleday Publishing Co., 1988.

Schiff, Aaron Wolfe, and Jackie Lee Schiff. "Passivity," *TAJ* 1:1.

Shephard, Sharon. "Television: The Prime Time Invader." *Christian Parenting Today*, September/October, 1989.

ENDNOTES

Introduction

1. "Grow up": According to a text note in the *NIV Study Bible*, the Greek for this phrase is the standard term for the desirable growth of children.
2. W. Penfield, "Memory Mechanisms," *Archives of Neurology and Psychiatry*, no. 67 (1952), pp. 178-198, with discussion by L. S. Kubiem, et al.
3. Eric Berne, MD, *Transactional Analysis in Psychotherapy* (New York: Grove Press, 1961), pp. 17,18,178-198.
4. W. Penfield and H. Jasper, *Epilepsy and the Functional Anatomy of the Brain* (Boston, MA: Little, Brown and Co., 1954), chapter XI; W. Penfield and L. Roberts, *Speech and Brain Mechanisms* (Princeton, NJ: Princeton University Press, 1959).
5. Doug Stringer, *Charisma* magazine (March 1999), p. 79.
6. Michael Rodgers and Marcus Losack, *Glendalough: A Celtic Pilgrimage* (Blackrock, C. Dublin: Columba Press, 1996), p. 112.
7. Leanne Payne, *The Healing Presence* (Grand Rapids, MI: Hamewith Books, 1995), p. 163.
8. Doug Stringer, "Pray Until Something Happens." http://www.synapsenow.com/ synapse/news/fullstory_public.cfm?articleid=17108&website=somebodycares houston.com.

Chapter 1: In the Beginning

1. Thomas Verny, *The Secret Life of the Unborn Child* (New York: Dell Publishing Co., 1981), pp. 15,23,67.
2. Ibid., p. 12.
3. Ibid., p. 19.
4. Ibid., pp. 38-39.
5. Ibid., pp. 13,16.
6. Ibid., pp. 13,17,49.
7. This is not always the reason for a baby to be breach; sometimes it is due to threatening conditions such as the placenta blocking the birth canal or the cord being wrapped around the baby's neck, to mention two possible causes. The possible physical reason should always be checked by your physician first. In these cases, the baby is right not to turn. However, if there is no medical or physical reason, the cause may be stress.
8. Verny, *The Secret Life of the Unborn Child*, pp. 78,81,95.
9. Ibid., pp. 16,17,27.
10. Ibid., pp. 74-76.
11. Ibid., pp. 87-90.
12. Ibid., p. 82.
13. Ibid., pp. 38-39.
14. Ibid., p. 30.
15. Frances MacNutt, *Praying for Your Unborn Child* (New York: Doubleday Publishing, 1988), pp. 1-3.
16. Verny, *The Secret Life of the Unborn Child*, pp. 76,80.
17. It is important to clarify that there can be other reasons for the oppression of perversion, including personal sin. Some other root causes that occur during development will be discussed in later chapters. However, the story here illustrates a cause not often considered and also a root cause for the oppression of perversion in some people.
18. Ibid., p. 13.
19. Ibid., pp. 16,48,50,63,89,98.

20. Ibid., p. 81.
21. Ibid., pp. 55-58.
22. Annie Murphy Paul, "The Womb, Your Mother, Yourself," *TIME* magazine, October 4, 2010, pp. 40-45.
23. "Vanishing Twin Syndrome," American Pregnancy Association, May 2007. http://www.americanpregnancy.org/multiples/vanishingtwin.html.

Chapter 2: Being

1. Jacqui and Aaron Schiff, "Passivity," *Transactional Analysis Journal*, vol. 1, no. 1 (1971), pp. 71-78.
2. Sandra Blakeslee, "Studies Show Talking with Infants Shapes Basis of Ability to Think," *New York Times* (April 17, 1997), p. D 21; Sharon Begley, "How to Build a Baby's Brain," *Newsweek Special Issue* (Spring/Summer 1997), pp. 28-32; Renee Baillargeon, "How Do Infants Learn About the Physical World?" *Current Directions in Psychological Science* (October 1994), pp. 1331-1340; Kathleen McAuliffe, "Making of a Mind," *Omni* (October 1985), pp. 62-66,74; Jacqui Schiff et al., *Cathexis Reader* (New York: Harper and Row, 1975); Paul Chance, "Your Child's Self-Esteem," *Parents Magazine Enterprises* (January 1982).
3. F. Rebelsky and C. Hanks, "Father's Verbal Interactions with Infants in the First Three Months of Life," *Child Development* (1971), pp. 42,63-68; Paul Roberts, "Father's Time," *Psychology Today* (May/June 1996), pp. 48-55,81.
4. Rene Spitz, "Hospitalization, Genesis of Psychiatric Conditions in Early Childhood," *Psychoanalytic Study of the Child*, vol. 1 (1945), pp. 53-74; W. Goldfarb, "Psychological Privation in Infancy and Subsequent Adjustment," *American Journal of Orthopsychiatry*, vol. 15 (1945), pp. 247-255; S. Provence and R. Lipton, *Children in Institutions* (New York: International Universities Press, 1962); Barry M. Lester, "There's More to Crying than Meets the Ear," *Childhood Newsletter*, vol. 2, no. 2 (1983).

Chapter 3: Exploration

1. J. Madeleine Nash, "Fertile Minds," *TIME* magazine (March 2, 1997), p. 54.
2. L. Joseph Stone and Joseph Church, *Childhood and Adolescence* (New York: Random House, 1984), pp. 212-214.
3. Nash, "Fertile Minds," p. 51.
4. Ibid.
5. Stone and Church, *Childhood and Adolescence,* pp. 212-214.
6. Sharon Begley, "Your Child's Brain," *Newsweek* (February 19, 1996), pp. 55-62.
7. The symbiotic bond between the mother and child becomes stronger month by month, reaching its strongest at eight months and then gradually diminishing in the months that follow. Separation from the mother in these first months is problematic for the child, and in the seventh to eighth month it can be traumatic.
8. Stone and Church, *Childhood and Adolescence,* p. 215.
9. J. H. Kennell and M. H. Klaus, eds., *Birth, Interaction and Attachment* (Skillman, NJ: Johnson and Johnson), pp. 35-43.
10. E. Fenichel, *Learning Through Supervision and Mentorship to Support the Development of Infant, Toddler and Their Families, Zero-Three* (1991), Annual Editions: Human Development (Guilford, CT: Dushkin Publishing, 1996-97).
11. Stone and Church, *Childhood and Adolescence,* pp. 285-287.

Chapter 4: Beginning Independence

1. Bernice Weissbourd, "The Myth of the Terrible Twos: Rethinking Toddlers' Bad Rap (As They Grow: 2 Years)," *Parents Magazine* (October 1995), 70 n. 10, 77(2).
2. Nancy Samalin, "How to Love Your Child, Even When You're Angry," *Family Circle* (April 1996), 24 n. 5(2).

3. James and Mary Kenny, "Punishment Won't Make Your Kids Good," *U.S. Catholic* (July 1996), 26 v. 61, n. 7(5); Nick Gallo, "Why Spanking Takes the Spunk Out of Kids," *Child* (March 1996), pp. 103,146-147; "Public Spanking: Is It an Answer to Teen Crime?" *Current Events* (March 11, 1996), 95, n. 21, 3(1); Ellen Wlody, "To Spank or Not to Spank?" *American Baby* (November 1995), 57, n. 11, 56(5); "Dr. Spock's Guide to Effective Discipline," *Parenting* (June/July 1995), 9 n. 5, 58(6); Nancy Samalin, "What's Wrong with Spanking?" *Parents' Magazine* (May 1995), 70 n. 5, 35(2); William Sears and Martha Sears, "8 Reasons Spanking Doesn't Work . . . and 5 Kinds of Techniques That Do," *Redbook* (March 1995), 184 n. 5, 156; "Sparing the Rod to Save the Child" (Corporal Punishment in the United Kingdom) (editorial), *New Statesman and Society* (June 24, 1994), 7 n. 308, 5(1); Hans-Joachim Heil, "Ein missverstandener Begriff: 'Zuchtigung'—was soll denn das?" *Der Auftrag*, Nr 61 (Dezember 1996), 58.

Chapter 5: Identity

1. L. Joseph Stone and Joseph Church, *Childhood and Adolescence* (New York: Random House, 1984), pp. 333-416.

2. Ibid.

3. Note: This story is a composite of several women's stories and in no way reflects any one incident or person. See Appendix A: Breaking Generational Curses.

Chapter 6: Gifts and Callings

1. L. Joseph Stone and Joseph Church, *Childhood and Adolescence* (New York: Random House, 1984), pp. 419-495.

2. Barrie Thorn, *Gender Play: Girls and Boys in School* (Piscataway, NJ: Rutgers University Press, 1993), pp. 27-47.

3. Sharon Begley, "How to Build a Baby's Brain," *Newsweek* (Spring/Summer 1997), pp. 28-32.

Chapter 7: Integrating, Connecting, Maturing

1. Pamela Levin, *Becoming the Way We Are* (Deerfield Beach, FL: Health Communications, Inc., 1988), p. 74.

2. Jay Giedd, "Inside the Teenage Brain," *Frontline*, PBS. http://www.pbs.org/wgbh/pages/frontline/shows/teenbrain/interviews/giedd.html#ixzz1XNjAvRAd.

3. David Elkind, *A Sympathetic Understanding of the Child*, 3rd edition (Needham Heights, MA: Allyn & Bacon, 1994), pp. 232,235-236.

4. Cesar G. Soriano and Michelle Hatty, "Eat or Die," *USA Weekend* (February 1998), pp. 20-22.

5. Deirdra Price, PhD, "About Eating Disorders, Facts and Figures," *Diet Free Solutions*. http://www.dietfreesolution.com/dfs/disorder.htm.

6. Ibid.

7. "What Is an Eating Disorder?" *Eating Disorder Recovery Online*. http://www.edrecovery.com/information.html; Price, "About Eating Disorders, Facts and Figures," p. 2.

8. Ibid.

9. "What Is an Eating Disorder?" *Eating Disorder Recovery Online*.

Chapter 8: Discovering God-Given Destiny

1. David Elkind, *A Sympathetic Understanding of the Child*, 3rd edition (Needham Heights, MA: Allyn & Bacon, 1994), pp. 242-246.

2. Ibid., pp. 246-251.

Chapter 9: Natural Development and Spiritual Development

1. According to a text note in the *NIV Study Bible*, the Greek for "grow up" is the standard term for the desirable growth of children.

Appendix B: Control Brings Life or Brings Death

1. Stephen R. Covey, *Seven Habits of an Effective Leader* (New York: Simon & Schuster, 1990), p. 39.